Positioning Yourself as an Expert

Positioning Yourself
as an Expert:

How Savvy Entrepreneurs
Become Credible Authorities

Compiled by
Connie Ragen Green

Edited by Geoff Hoff

Copyright © 2014 by Hunter's Moon Publishing
Crown Image © Sashkin - Fotolia.com

ISBN: 978-1-937988-11-1

Hunter's Moon Publishing

Table of Contents

Introduction

By Connie Ragen Green

When people first began talking to me about gaining expert status and becoming an authority in my niche back in 2006, I felt like I would never know enough about anything to be considered as such. They had to mean someone else. Here I was, a former classroom teacher who had also worked as a real estate broker and residential appraiser, trying to make a name for myself on the Internet. Certainly people would see that I knew less about business and other topics of great importance than could fill a thimble. Obviously my self-esteem and confidence were at an all-time low, and that would have to change if I were to build the lucrative online business I was dreaming of at that time.

Soon I came to realize that every single one of us have extensive knowledge on a variety of topics based on our personal interests, education, work history, and life experiences and that all of this can easily be channeled into positioning ourselves as experts and authorities in our chosen field and niche. My twenty years of working in the classroom in two inner city schools helped me to garner information that I otherwise would never have known about so many things related to teaching in the public school system, bilingual education, and serving children with special needs. Years of working in the real estate and appraisal industry helped me to amass knowledge that continues to help me with my own finances and property holdings.

You are an expert in *at least* one area, and it is up to you to position yourself that way when you are building your online business. Stand tall and know that you alone can serve others with your specialized knowledge and that you can attain a level of fame and fortune when you are willing to share what you know with others.

I think back to my first year as a teacher. A fifth grader named Eric was having some problems at school and his parents made an appointment to speak with me after school. They asked me all kinds of questions about what they should do at home to help him succeed at school, and my first thought was that they should know better than I would about this because they had known him for ten years and I'd just met him a couple of weeks earlier. But the truth was that they already saw me as the expert, and once I caught up with this idea psychologically I was able to make suggestions based on my experiences as a parent, my training as a teacher, and even my limited classroom experience. By winter break Eric's grades, behavior, and attitude had all improved, and I had assumed the role of expert educator that his parents had already acknowledged.

What about you? How is your online business related to your previous experiences? I believe that we all choose a niche, at least initially, that is directly related to some part of our past. This is where you will have what I refer to as 'crossover skills' that will help you to make the transition into becoming a successful online entrepreneur.

For example, my first niche was in helping people to write, publish, and market eBooks on their topics. This was based on my years of experience helping students from Kindergarten through high school to put their thoughts, ideas, and experiences into writing for their assignments. It was also an excellent way for me to break into the world of online marketing while helping others to achieve their goals of becoming published authors. Along the way I learned so much from serving those who had come to me as a trusted advisor to guide them through the writing, publishing, and marketing process.

This book is filled with stories from entrepreneurs who have positioned themselves as experts in a variety of areas. Learn from them, and visit their main sites to find out even more about them. The insight they are sharing with you here will help you to catapult yourself to expert status very quickly. My goal is to share what has worked, as well as what we will all be doing in the near future to expand our reach and leverage the power of the Internet to grow our businesses exponentially.

To Your Massive Success!
Connie Ragen Green
http://ConnieRagenGreen.com

An Expert in 21 Quick, Easy Lessons!

By Ed Manske

On the internet, your ticket to success is authority. Everyone is looking for experts to be their best source of information. Do you go to the search engines looking for bad websites, full of poor writing, produced by those who have less knowledge than you? Of course not. You search for sites that clearly and fully answer your questions, written by experts who are capable of teaching those exact subjects.

How does anyone become an expert in anything? Is it luck or is it magic? Is it hard work spent over a long period of time? Or is it something else that looks a little like both of these? Has it occurred to you that anyone who becomes expert at anything first makes the decision to learn as much as possible about a particular topic? I like to think of gaining expertise, and becoming well known for it, as another example of the adage that the harder I work, the luckier I get.

Nothing comes without effort, but becoming an expert, or authority figure, is very much like anything else you want to accomplish. There are simple, straightforward steps that you can learn and follow that will lead you to this goal. My purpose in this article is to show you these steps and procedures in an easy to grasp way so you, too, can become an expert in your chosen niche in almost no time at all.

Let's look at the important reasons for choosing to become an expert before we actually proceed with the lessons. I'm going to use the Internet as the vehicle for your expert / authority training since I suspect most people reading this are most interested in just that.

People trust experts. People are always seeking the best informed teachers they can find. People don't necessarily believe or value your information and opinions if you're not seen as an expert.

Experts attract attention online, in media and in person. Blog posts by experts tend to draw more responses and comments. People want to develop a connection with authority figures and share their ideas with the experts.

The media frequently wants to interview experts. All media, including newspaper, radio, TV and Internet, want to access expertise to provide accurate, quality content for their reporting assignments. Being a visible and available authority in your subject niche makes you a prime candidate for these media contacts. The various media also want experts to write articles, columns and commentaries directly for publication. Guest posting on websites is yet another method to display mastery of specialized knowledge to target audiences.

These days, virtually every seminar and conference promoter wants top experts to lead their events. Expert presentations dramatically increase attendance at these events and add tremendous credibility for their attendees. People like to meet popular experts in person.

Experts want to meet and confer with other experts. Experts are attracted to other experts and want to create joint ventures, collaborations and the opportunities to grow each other's audiences through these introductions. Experts want to share good information, contacts and content with their peers.

Expert articles get more links. Since incoming links are one of the important determinants for SEO rankings, and being an authority in your specialty makes it much easier to gain great natural links from other important sites, experts often achieve the top search engine page results.

Expanding social media contact is easier for experts. It's a natural! People want to be connected to experts. They want to follow leaders in any subject and enjoy the prestige of their affiliation with experts.

Experts generate more and better ideas for product and content creation. This happens by virtue of the fact that they possess a broader, deeper knowledge of their niche and its nuances.

Experts predict new trends and help prepare students to grow with the resulting changes. You can't predict everything, but you will know what things are likely to happen in your particular niche area.

People want to buy from experts. A majority of people rightly believe that experts recognize the highest quality and value in products and services. Since buyers want the most for their money, they naturally want to purchase things created or recommended by experts whose opinions they consider trustworthy and relevant.

People want to work with experts. Authorities typically draw the best talent to their organizations. The smart, hard working candidates for positions as employees or contractors are eager to be involved with the leaders in every field. This can be a huge advantage to the success and productivity of any business.

Expert articles, blog posts, social media comments, tweets and content syndications often spread through the Internet like wildfire. Viral distribution of anything pertaining to expert know-how is extremely common. People enjoy finding and sharing new, interesting and authoritative material as a way to show their own awareness of important content. They get a form of expert elbow rubbing and recognition by spreading the good word!

Next, let's explore the specific steps to achieving expertise and gaining authority.

1. Select your expertise niche. It's much easier and faster to study a subject you already know something about and enjoy than something you find difficult and boring. Pick something you love and you'll readily develop passion for your chosen topic. That's important because your enthusiasm will show through and your audience will recognize your knowledge and expertise more rapidly.

2. You must develop the authority to know precisely what you're talking about, and gain the skills to express and

teach those subjects well. So what's the key to that? Very simply, knowledge of your niche.

Knowing your subject matter cold is the starting point in your pursuit of expert status. Spend as much time as possible to acquire the knowledge that will make you an expert in that area. Once achieved, content creation, which is the essence of internet authority, becomes much easier since you'll actually know your subject completely.

In other words, you, the teacher, need to know more than your students do. You don't need to master all the information in the universe, but you do need to able to provide the answers to their questions. You also need to be able to identify the situations where you will consult outside resources for answers you don't already know. You need to know enough that the information and perspective you share with your audience is new and valuable to them. Learn to help people get what they need and want from you.

3. Blog about and discuss your subject. Start immediately and you'll be accomplishing three important things. You'll be learning to research and create information about your niche, you'll be gaining knowledge to add to your authority and you'll be displaying your results to an audience interested in your topic. The more people who know what you provide, the sooner you'll be recognized for your contributions.

4. Present yourself as a professional and an authority. On the web and in your personal appearances you must put your best foot forward. No one will accept you as an expert if you don't look and act the part. Use your best effort to produce high quality information and education for your followers. Be

aware, also, of the impression you make on your audience. Use a good personal appearance to your advantage in crafting your authority.

5. Link to and refer to other experts. Identify other teachers you respect and enjoy. Learn from them and link to them. By doing this you will be recognized as someone with the talent to appreciate high quality content. You'll be seen as someone who knows excellence when they see it and, perhaps, you'll earn the attention of these other experts as well as links back from them.

6. Guest blog to extend your reach. Offer to write content and comments on other blogs in your chosen area of expertise. This guest blogging helps the blog host to supply an interesting variety of information and opinion to their readers. It helps you to gain a reputation for your abilities with a new, previously untapped, audience.

7. Teach a class. The best method to learn your topic quickly is to teach others about it. The preparation will force you to separate the important and significant concepts of your niche from the things that don't really matter. The questions you'll get from your students will tell you what's meaningful to them. Your teaching can be online or in person. It won't make any difference. The sooner you do it, though, the sooner people will be able learn from you what you already know.

8. Begin your speaking career now. Again, whether you talk to your audience on audio or video recordings or in person won't matter. The crucial thing is that you start doing

it. People want to feel a personal connection to their experts and one of the simplest ways to make that happen is for them to hear your voice. It gives them a sense of exactly who you are and what you know. In addition, a mastery of this type of public speaking will give you increased authority just because so many others hesitate and procrastinate to take this step.

9. Create audio or video podcasts. Create training videos or short topic how-to videos and post them on You Tube. Do a weekly iTunes podcast in your specialty niche area and tie it into your regular blogging websites. Produce content that breaks long or complicated procedures into easy step by step operations for your students. Turn something dull and tedious into something engaging and thought provoking. Your audience will see and hear these channels and the perception of your authority status will increase exponentially.

10. Arrange to speak at a local college or give speaking presentations at service organizations, associations or clubs without charge, of course. The public exposure you receive from these events will confirm your growing authority with an ever larger audience.

11. Become a member of a trade association where you can display your expertise and offer your content writing or speaking services. See if they need someone to write a column for the magazine or newsletter. Always include your contact information in anything you write for the organization. Also include your web address so that the members can follow you to your internet home and connect with a respected authority in the industry - you!

12. Sponsor a booth at a trade show involved with your specialty niche. Speak at an event, run for a position on your association's board or volunteer to serve on a committee. To gain more fantastic visibility and credibility become active in whatever industry organizations represent people looking for your type of expertise.

13. Prepare and send out press releases either locally or online. Include your credentials and a short biography with a press release pertaining to any event or other item of interest to your audience. You can promote your activities by using the online press release services or by manually creating and sending your releases. The more you promote, the more well-known you become.

14. Create content and products that display your finest work. Becoming an expert is very closely related to becoming a content creation machine. One can't exist without the other. Articles, blogs, seminars, webinars, live presentations, books, podcasts and videos are only some of the types of content that you can create. Any content is an example of the expert level of skill you possess and will further promote your status as an authority.

15. Study the advertisements placed by other experts. This is the fastest method to learn about their new products. Experts in any field always stay on top of information about new developments and products. Product launches, new technologies and growing movements within a subject niche are often seen first in advertisements. This may occur,

sometimes, even before they appear in media reporting or other content discussions. Knowledge of everything that's going on and exciting in an area is definitely another clear indication of your expertise.

16. Present your own conference, seminar or webinar and build additional recognition for your credentials. Since experts are in high demand to lead all kinds of events, why not produce your own? As we've previously discussed, people want to attend events with expert leaders and instructors. By organizing conferences, seminars or webinars you can attract an audience specifically interested in your subject area. You may even decide to invite other experts to join you in presenting at your event. Your exposure in a peer group of such authorities will work to confer even more expert status for you.

17. Connect with real people in many different ways. There are many compelling reasons to position yourself as an expert, not the least of which is that people want to do business with authorities they know, like and trust. The starting point for all this is discovery. People must find you to begin the entire process. Make it easy for your audience to find you! Be available to them in a variety of ways. Attend events, comment on blog posts, do Meetups, network with everyone online and at live conferences. Be active on social media like Facebook, LinkedIn and Twitter and pay attention to the feedback! Go where the people are - accessible authorities beat hidden secrets every time.

18. Make quality your prime target in everything you do. Nothing reveals your expert status more than giving your best performance in all projects you undertake. Finish all your work, on schedule, by the time to which you have agreed. This quote, I think, from Alistair Cooke expresses it extremely well: "A professional is someone who can do his best work when he doesn't feel like it."

19. Learn constantly. Always strive to learn more about your niche topic and always be ready to update your skills. According to Denis Waitley, you should "Never become so much of an expert that you stop gaining expertise. View life as a continuous learning experience." Once you become an accepted authority in anything, your education never ends.

20. Seize every opportunity to improve your authority reputation. Whenever the circumstances allow you to share your experience and knowledge with interested groups, do it - especially if doing so can help to further establish your credentials as an expert. Someone once said that the real definition of an expert is someone who knows a topic so thoroughly well that they can admit how much they still have to learn about it.

21. Don't be afraid to be wrong. Study your subject carefully to be as accurate as possible, but don't hesitate to form your own opinions and judgments. Adopting your own theories is a clear indication of your true authority. Strong, and sometimes controversial, belief systems are the trademark of many well received experts.

In closing, earning the badge of expertise and authority is an amazingly valuable tool in any endeavor. Please remember these two quotes to help you remember these lessons. "Unless you're the lead dog on the sled team, the view never changes," and as W Clement Stone said, "Try, try, try, and keep on trying is the rule that must be followed to become an expert in anything."

Ed has been selling and training sales champions for over 30 years. A student of Zig Ziglar, Joe Girard, Brian Tracy, Tom Hopkins and Bert Kuptz, Ed is originally from the Milwaukee / Chicago area. Ed has been under-promising and over-delivering in the real estate, banking, financial, insurance, manufacturing, restaurant, auto sales, direct selling, trade show and internet marketing industries longer than he likes to admit. In 2000 he and his lovely bride, Michelle, moved to Las Vegas and was finally able to stop shoveling Midwestern snow.

Currently, he spends his time helping students apply classic sales and marketing methods to their internet marketing businesses. His "Island of Entrepreneurship" sales philosophy trains aspiring online marketers to maximize their sales results by conquering any sales reluctance and demolishing any fear of selling.

Expert in Italy

By Maria Lassila

When I arrived in Italy in November of 2000 from Southern California, I felt like the anti-expert in everything. I couldn't speak the language, I didn't understand how anything worked, and I was continually frustrated when I tried to use my American point of view to make sense of my new world in Milan. Before I made the move, it hadn't really sunk in that every single thing was going to be different from what I was used to, but it quickly became clear to me once I landed. I looked to those around me for help, grateful to every individual who helped me solve each problem. In retrospect, I realize that everyone starts at level zero of knowledge and experience and that expertise is something you acquire, sometimes without even being aware of it.

As an American expatriate living here now for more than a decade, I am considered to have three areas of expertise just for being here this long – with varying degrees of accuracy. One day it dawns on you that the reason why others gravitate toward you is because you have good information and that you share it in useful ways. That's what happened to me.

To the Italians I interact with here, I am the expert on all things American (just to clarify, over here that means being from the US – apologies to continental neighbors from Canada and Mexico). First and foremost, that means apologist/explainer-in-chief for anything the US government does – election miscounts, gun laws (or lack thereof), debt cliff stand-offs, etc. I'm constantly quizzed about why "my" government is engaging in its behavior and what the end result will look like. Never mind that I can't explain it to myself, let alone to an outside observer. The second most popular topic is American food – both types and quantities. No, I don't eat a heaping plate of eggs, bacon and hash browns every morning, nor do most of my US friends and family. Yes, US restaurants often serve individual portions large enough for small groups.

To those stateside who I encounter on my frequent trips back, I am the expert on all things Italian. Explaining the political situation is less of an exercise in embarrassment now that Berlusconi is no longer in charge, but it doesn't make it any easier. Not having grown up in the system, I don't know that I'll ever be able to completely wrap my head around the Italian process, let alone be able to convey much beyond the basics to others. Luckily, the subject is easily changed to the less complicated one of Italian food, a topic that is decidedly easier to discuss with certainty and confidence. I am happy to expound on the reasons why the Italian cuisine is so wonderful. I am less happy when I am inevitably coerced into eating in an Italian restaurant in the US and then being asked how it compares with what I eat "back home" – the expectation usually being that this particular restaurant is in fact truly authentic. Unfortunately, it is rarely the case: often it's very good in its own way, just not very Italian.

The third "automatic expert" status is the one I hold with other expatriates. Those recently arrived especially consider me to be able to demystify everything about how to integrate and make the most of their experience here. This is the expert status I have actively sought and am building upon to become known as an expert on visibility among other locals. What is my strategy?

The first step was to find and join professional networking associations that attracted members from the expatriate community. As these groups tend to be always desperate for help, I immediately volunteered to help the organizers and within a short time became officially part of their committees. Having a title instantly elevates you in others' perceptions. When I'm having a conversation with someone and they ask my role in the association, "I'm the vice president" always evokes a positive reaction and increase in friendly interest. Suddenly, everything I say carries more weight; often the person will point me out to others. It doesn't seem to matter what the title is, just the official connection - I say this having held various positions over the years.

Helping to manage events for these groups has given me four key opportunities to connect with participants.

1) Answering pre-event emails during the online registration period establishes me as the person to look for upon arrival.

2) Welcoming attendees at the registration desk allows me to connect directly with individuals as they arrive, putting names and faces together.

3) Being the person with the microphone: opening the event with an official welcome, introducing speakers, and facilitating networking exercises. This role instantly conveys expertise: as the person emceeing, I am obviously in charge with the experience and background to back me up.

4) Following up post-event with an evaluation survey reinforces me as the face of the group and opens up dialogue by encouraging them to contact me with questions or suggestions.

Contacting speakers for events for the networking groups is another way I position myself. I'm a decision-maker, choosing who will speak and on what topic, providing them a platform while simultaneously offering access to great content to those who attend to hear the presentation.

I started my own podcast featuring interviews with other expatriate business owners and professionals in Milan. Just the fact of launching and hosting a podcast makes me an expert to others. The technical aspects can seem daunting to the average person: how to start, what tools you need for recording and editing, how to get it posted on a website. Of course, the reality is that a podcast is a project like any other. You do the research to see what it will entail, you invest in the training and equipment – whether that means paying someone for help or spending your time seeking and gathering information on your own – and then you start. Those are intimidating obstacles to many, which means I stand out for having accomplished them. When I ask people if I can interview them, I let them know that my podcast is on iTunes which means they will have the added visibility of being found there as well as on my blog. They are always impressed, imagining how it would feel to find themselves there.

I'm currently working on a book, since nothing says expert like "published author." In this spirit, I have already contributed to other books, including this one. Publishing a first book is great, but it's even better to be associated with other books as well. The fact that I was asked to contribute by other authors demonstrates that I am respected by others in my field.

What else is in my future plans? My next step will be to take action on increasing my visibility online. There are so many opportunities in social media that it takes a while to optimize all the pertinent ones, but concentrating on my blog and LinkedIn makes the most sense for me as a priority. I'm told that the most important thing to keep in mind is that small ordinary actions done on a regular basis will result in huge extraordinary results, so my most valuable act is to keep moving forward.

Maria Lassila is an online visibility strategist, podcast host, author and networking maven living in Milan, Italy, for more than a decade since her transplant from the west coast of the U.S. (Washington state and then southern California). For 20 years she worked in the apparel industry, ranging from retail sales to managing production for luxury brands in ladies' shoes and golfwear. Her current focus is on helping small businesses and independent professionals grow their visibility with the English-speaking community in Milan, both online and off. Read more at http://DoingBusinessInMilan.com

Create Your Path to Becoming an Expert

By Susan Guiher

"When you do not know a thing, to allow that
you do not know it-this is knowledge."
~Confucius

When considering the concept of what makes someone an expert, I considered all those whom I have considered an expert and the path they traveled and then I considered my own path to becoming an expert. I realized it often comes back to owning what you do know AND understanding what you still need to learn. As stated by Confucius, it is in the allowing of the learning that we obtain true knowledge.

So I will share with you my knowledge and my path toward becoming an expert with the understanding that I am still learning and will continue to do so long after this chapter is written. I charge you with continuing to learn in whatever are you are currently an expert or are seeking to become one.

From my experience, there are components that contribute to becoming an expert:

1) God-given skills and talents you are born with
2) Education
3) Experience

Most often you will use these in combination and ALL require hard work to become an expert.

Are you using your Skills and Talents?

I have found it interesting that the skills and talents that we are born with are the ones we tend to de-value, often even referring to them as "gifts". However, when we start from an area where we are naturally talented and expand upon that area, often we bring insights and thoughts that others don't.

In my case, I have several natural skills, such as listening and the ability to quickly "connect the dots", which allow me to learn new things quickly and to recognize trends. I have the natural ability to clarify and teach concepts to others.

I use my "gifts" every day when working with students.

Take a moment right now and think about your natural skills and talents. Are you naturally funny, able to cook a mouth-watering apple pie or hit a home run with ease? What did you do easily and with great abandon as a teenager? Often it is those talents that we can tap into as adults in our desire to achieve expert status.

So how/when does education fit in?

I have often heard the recommendation that "all you need to do is read 5 books on a topic and you are an expert on that topic." Now, I am not quite sure about that. What I think is that if you read 5 books on a topic, you will probably know a great deal more than most people about that topic and can share that knowledge with others; you may even be seen by others as "an expert on that topic."

The key to being an expert is continuing your education and sharing this knowledge with others. I am considered a Master at Communication. As I discussed earlier, I am naturally talented at listening both to what is said and what is left unsaid. I expanded upon this talent by getting degrees in Speech/language Pathology and Audiology (have a B.S and two Masters' Degrees in this field) and then continuing to study Adult Communication at the doctoral level. So education is very important.

However, even though I have studied a great in this field, I continue to learn more. I went through more than 800 hours of coach training (at four different schools) and continue to learn from others.

But education only truly matters if you use it and then share it with others. The teaching and sharing of what you know is what sets you apart from others as an expert in a particular area.

I began my career in the medical field and shared my knowledge with my patients and their families and then with colleagues and then taking on students. I always signed up with our university to take students for several reasons. First, it was a way for me to give back to a field and profession I deeply respected and loved. Secondly, it was a way of ensuring that my knowledge stayed current and that I kept learning, and lastly for me, it was a way of contributing to the professionalism and level of expertise of clinicians in the field. It was my goal to help create other experts.

Mentors: their importance and the need to choose wisely

As most experts do, I have always had mentors in my life, beginning with my first job as a Speech Pathologist. Cathy was an expert in the field, recognized for her expertise. The job I took was at the highly challenging Temple University Hospital in Philadelphia where I worked many long hours collaborating on cases with top-notch medical personnel. The pay-off was that I was exposed to situations where my clinical skill was tapped into, stretched rather quickly. Cathy taught me an incredible amount while also providing me opportunities to grow. Within three years, I had the expertise and experiences of therapists many years my senior and was able to move on to managing my own department and eventually into an executive role where I supervised more than 80 staff and made significant contributions to the field. Choosing the right mentors (and learning when I have chosen the wrong ones) has been incredibly important for me throughout my multiple careers and an important consideration when choosing your own mentor(s) (*yes you can have more than one if you choose carefully.*) When I left my corporate job to start my own business, I sought out, invested in and learned from mentors who could expand my knowledge and expertise in the areas of marketing, sales, coaching and consulting as well as writing and publishing.

When choosing a mentor, look for someone who has already achieved what you want to achieve, both professionally and personally. Do you want a specific lifestyle? Does the person you are looking for as a mentor have this lifestyle? Look for someone who is a powerful role model and willing to share their expertise and, preferably, their contacts with you. Mentors come in many shapes and sizes so look for someone who is the right fit for you and one you can communicate with openly about your needs and expectations. Lastly, don't take your mentor(s) for granted. Show appreciation and provide feedback as most mentors appreciate knowing how they have supported you and also enjoy sharing and celebrating your success. I recommend you keep in touch even when you move on beyond your mentors. Many can become trusted colleagues and perhaps collaborators as your expertise grows.

Declare your expert status

The first step to becoming known as an expert is actually declaring that you are one. Once I left my corporate job, I first identified my skills from that job and began to work with clients who needed those and as my expertise grew, I continued to expand what I could offer. Then, interestingly, as my expertise grew, my offerings actually narrowed. You see, I realized that I was an expert at growing businesses while also helping people have more time for family and themselves. It became my passion to help small business owners identify their greatness, step into that and then to understand what they needed to do to thrive as a business owner.

It is that passion that drives me and truly makes me an expert at what I do. It is a cycle, I tap into my natural skills as a master communicator and listener, and I enhance my education so that as I learn more, I have more to offer. And the more I have to offer, the more I share and the greater my expert status grows.

To sum it all up, in order to be an expert, you need to:

1) Tap into your natural talents
2) Get the education and training you need
3) Find and learn from mentors
4) SHARE your wisdom and expertise with others

It is the sharing and growing that make being an expert so rewarding.

Find out more about Sue Guiher at:
http://thrive4success.com.

Being an Expert

By Dr. Jeanette Cates

Which Type of Expert Are You?

Everyone claims to be an expert at some time in their career. Yet nothing harms your field of expertise more than when people claim to have expertise with nothing to back it up. This is a common occurrence in the online business world so I have seen a lot of overnight experts come and go in the 17 years I have been online. It is a disservice to the industry, as well as the client.

Generally when we think of an expert we assume that that person has long-term experience in their area of expertise. They may have studied it over a period of years, formally or informally. They may have certifications, degrees, awards, and other indicators that they are an "expert."

But I've recently recognized two types of expertise that you can claim. Both are valid and both can be used in positioning yourself as an expert.

Short-Term or Situational Expertise

There is a type of expertise that is rarely discussed, but often used. It is "short-term" expertise. It is often situational and brought on by a need for information. It is intensive and generally short-lived.

For example, if you are a new author who wants to publish on the Kindle platform, you have two choices: become a short-term expert or hire the expertise. Either way you can achieve the goal of publishing a book successfully.

If you choose to hire the expertise, you may hire a book coach, an editor, someone to format your book, someone else to create a cover. You may even hire someone to ghost-write the book for you. Essentially you don't need to know anything yourself, other than the goal you want to achieve and how to hire the best people for the job.

On the other hand, if you decide to become a short-term expert on Kindle publishing, you will most likely

- take a course (or two)
- read multiple articles
- watch a few videos or webinars
- talk to multiple people who are already doing it
- perhaps hire a coach to walk you through the steps
- study the marketplace in your topic area
- examine other Kindle books in your topic area

- buy several Kindle books on how to publish a Kindle book

In short, by the time you publish your book on Kindle, you will have become an expert on doing so!

Limited Range

Short-term expertise, however, is situational. While you have gained the expertise to publish your book on Kindle, you haven't broadened your scope. At this point claiming to be a Kindle publishing expert would be premature.

On the other hand, if you published multiple books of your own you would expand your knowledge of techniques. By the third or fourth book, you would have developed a system for publishing Kindle books. You would have checklists, procedures, and a group of resources that you have gathered to make the task easier. In short, you would be an expert in publishing a variety of your own books.

Are you ready to claim that you are a Kindle publishing expert yet? Not really. In order to do that, you will need to apply your system to other people's books. If it works for other people's writing, for fiction, and non-fiction, in a variety of genres, then you are ready to claim expertise as a Kindle publishing expert.

Of course, by the time you reach that level of expertise, you will have spent quite a bit of time on the tasks involved. You will have read hundreds of articles and tested the information for yourself. You will have gained a lot of experience, in multiple different situations. You will understand what works and what doesn't and when each is likely to occur. In short, you will have become a long-term expert in the topic.

Long-Term Expertise

How does short-term expertise differ from long-term expertise? There are actually three factors that differentiate which type of expertise you possess.

Length of Time You Have Studied This Topic

This is the most easily observable and therefore the most frequently used measure of expertise. Someone who has been a master of a topic for multiple years is generally considered an "expert." By virtue of the fact that they have done it over a long period of time, it makes them a long-term expert.

But naturally just studying something for many years does not automatically make you an expert. You may have a lot of knowledge, but until you actually apply that knowledge, you are just a smart reader of the topic.

Likewise, a short period of intense study may equate to more casual study over a longer period. For example, in the Kindle publishing example above you could study intensely for a week and publish a single book, yet still not be an expert. So time alone is not the determinant.

Depth of Your Understanding

Generally the longer you study a topic, the deeper you go into the topic. Consider the Doctoral Theses written about Shakespeare from 1990 to 1995. There were 55 different dissertations - on just that one author! And that is only from the universities in the United Kingdom.

To write a dissertation of several hundred pages on one aspect of Shakespeare's writing takes a very deep understanding of the topics related to the study of Shakespeare.

That is the depth of understanding we usually associate with a long-term expert. The same could be true of a WordPress programmer, for example. His or her depth of understanding of the code, operating system, and levels of detail indicate a depth of understanding of a long-term expert. But just understanding that one topic in depth, but in isolation, does not create expertise.

Breadth of Understanding

Knowledge in any field does not operate in a vacuum. Just as the WordPress expert must understand multiple levels of operating systems and programming languages and how they interact, the Shakespeare expert must understand the historical context, the cultural norms, and the nuances of language.

This breadth of understanding comes with experience and in-depth study. It is not quickly acquired. That's why generally someone who has studied a topic over a long period possesses both depth and breadth of knowledge.

In addition to depth and breadth providing a deeper understanding, the long view of a topic adds the historical context. The more you understand the history of a topic and how it has evolved over the years, the greater your understanding of how the pieces impact one another.

For example, for years we were uncertain whether someone who did not use a computer programming language could understand how a website worked. Now it's a given that few people can program, but everyone can use a computer. However, those who do have a programming knowledge have a deeper understanding of why things work or don't work on your computer. If they have been doing it for many years, they understand why we do things as we do and the alternatives. It's the breadth and depth and history combined with the long term that provide a true expert.

One Bite at a Time

Can a short-term expert compare to a long-term expert on a given topic? Yes, as long as the topic is limited in depth and breadth. That's where the difference arises.

Consider an apple as the long-term expert's level of knowledge. He or she understands that apple - where it came from, how it grew, what factors controlled the growth, how it reproduces, what goes into the flavor, all the possible uses of that apple.

The short term expert understands the bite they took - how big it is, what it tastes like. But they don't know where it fits in the whole apple. The short-term expert's knowledge may be good - on that single bite.

30

And because their knowledge is not designed to be long-term, a short-term expert's expertise will expire over the long haul, if they do not keep up. Should they choose to maintain their knowledge in this newfound area, they can move into the realm of long-term expert, as they add time, breadth and depth of knowledge.

When You Need Each Type of Expert

If you need to hire an expert, you may choose either type, as long as you recognize the limitations of a short-term expert. If you need the specific area of knowledge that he or she possesses, a short-term expert may be the perfect choice.

However, if you need to look at the big picture, make strategic decisions, or choose a long-term course of action, the long-term expert should be your only choice. Only they provide the breadth and depth of knowledge required to make big decisions.

Where You Can Claim Each Type of Expertise

As the expert, it is up to you to recognize your limitations and be honest about them. If you have only published your own books, tell others who are considering hiring you that you are happy to work with them, although you have only done your own books to this point. If you are still learning a process, explain that you are not yet an expert, but will put in the time and effort necessary to help them achieve their goal while you expand on your expertise.

On the other hand, when you are an expert, don't be shy about claiming it. Do not wait for "permission." No one is going to come along and anoint you as an expert, unless you take the time to get a formal education in the topic. Most business people don't have time for that nowadays and it's not required in most fields.

Instead, recognize what you are a short-term expert on and where you have long-term expertise. As long as you recognize what type of expertise you are claiming or what type of expert you are hiring, you will be able to avail yourself of both types of expertise.

Dr. Jeanette Cates is the best-selling author of more than 10 books and is considered a Kindle publishing expert with short-term expertise. She writes books to help readers leverage their expertise, including teaching online, writing their own books, and building an online business. You can follow Jeanette on social media and her blog at http://JeanetteCates.com

What is an Expert?

By Debbie O'Grady

Dictionaries and encyclopedias generally agree. Let me summarize: An expert is someone who is recognized as a source of advice because of demonstrated knowledge or skill gained from education, training, practice, or experience.

I imagine that fine tuning this definition might depend on which side of the expertise you are looking from. Are there people you know that you think of as an expert? Do you consider yourself an expert? Do you see that the definition of expert may be different for yourself than for another person you regard as an expert? I know it was for me, for a long time, until I realized that an expert is really just someone who knows a lot about a particular subject and it didn't really matter where they got the information from - formal education or life experience. Once I realized that, I started noticing that there are a lot of experts on a lot of different subjects out there and I was one of them. So, if anyone might be considered an expert in their chosen field, what are the specific things a person can do to be noticed and stand out from every other expert in that same field? That is exactly what I am going to share with you in this chapter. I will describe my experiences and the different things I have done in the past to be considered an expert. Some of these things worked very well, and some did not. I will share that information too. I will close with a final bit of information concerning what I will be doing in the future - some new things and some I have done before. Things I will continue to do to position myself as an expert.

First let me introduce myself.

"Queen of Accountability"

My name is Debbie O'Grady and if we have met in the last five years, virtually or in person, and depending on where or when we met, you may know me as a consultant, a mentor, a trainer or a coach. I still do all of these things. Plus, I have recently accepted the title of "Queen of Accountability". This title encompasses most all the roles I've held and performed throughout my life and career, both in Corporate America and, now, as an Entrepreneur and Business Coach. No matter what my job description was, I tended to support and watch out for my colleagues and teammates, to help ensure each individual accomplished his or her goals – be they life or work goals. The title "Queen of Accountability" was bestowed on me by my coaches and clients and I've accepted it with honor and as a compliment of the highest value.

I am an Accountability Coach, and I work with individuals who want to stay focused to accomplish their goals. I also work with coaches who want to add accountability to their existing programs to help their clients succeed in the quickest way possible.

My expertise in accountability pretty much grew out of necessity. I did not take any courses in college that pertained to accountability, or do tons of research around the topic. I will admit that my Master's degree in Systems Management provides a solid background for managing, motivating, and encouraging people to do their best work.

My experience as a manager in corporate America taught me the importance of mentoring and coaching. Especially, mentoring and coaching the members of my team. I learned how to help people identify and cultivate their strengths; to extend and broaden their outlooks; to stretch for their goals and be the best they could be. Often, better than they thought they could be. I felt I did things a bit differently from the other managers because I didn't wait for yearly reviews to measure how each person on my team was doing in achieving his or her career goals. Instead I requested accountability on a more frequent schedule, so each person could review and assess the progress they were making towards accomplishing the goals they had set for themselves. Without that frequent accountability, their longer term goals tended to be forgotten and sometimes even lost with all the day-to-day distractions and emergent challenges needing to be handled. It was great to see a greater percentage of my team get promoted and take on challenging new positions.

When I left corporate America to start my own business as a Consultant, I learned to hold my clients accountable for the actions needed to achieve the levels of performance excellence they aspired to, and to produce the evidence I needed to complete the work they hired me for. It required a lot of tact on my part because they were, after all, my clients. I found most of the motivational techniques I used when working with junior members of my team worked just as well with my clients because they too wanted to succeed and see their companies prosper.

Now I've transitioned my business from consulting for corporate clients, assessing and telling them how well they've done, to focusing on helping my clients do better, with business coaching, specializing in Accountability coaching. I use the expertise I developed and honed throughout the years to help Entrepreneurs accomplish their goals (both personal and business), and thereby build and grow their business.

Positioning myself as an expert

You can see how, through the years, each new role I undertook allowed me to expand my knowledge and expertise so that, today, I am considered an expert in my chosen field of Accountability Coaching. So, what are some of the things I do to gain visibility as an expert in Accountability so more people will know me as the true "Queen of Accountability"?

The very first thing I've done is to create my Signature Statement so I can briefly explain what I do whenever someone asks. Here is how I answer the question "So, what do you do?"

"You know how people join a coaching program specifically to get the help they need to accomplish their goals, but after a while they find it's just not happening as fast as they'd hoped, or even not at all?

"Well, I offer Accountability Programs to help people stay focused and moving forward to accomplish their goals in the time they desire and often much quicker than they'd ever expected.

"My Accountability Programs can help individuals whether they already have a coach or not and are a valuable complement for Coaches who want to provide the benefits of Accountability to their clients within their existing programs."

I also attend networking events and live training and conferences where I can meet people and talk about what I offer. You can see why creating my Signature Statement had to be my very first step. Without a way to quickly describe what I do (and specifically define my expertise), the people I meet at these events would not know.

Of course attending events and networking is just the beginning, the tip of the iceberg, for what you can do to position yourself as an expert in your chosen field. Some of the other things I do are to train or deliver presentations at both live and virtual events. My topics focus on accountability, as well as productivity and efficiency, which are products that result from leveraging accountability to succeed.

Once you establish yourself as a presenter at others' events, the next step is to host your own events. I have done this virtually, using teleseminars and webinars, to train people how to plan out the action steps needed to accomplish their goals. It is during these training sessions that I introduce and describe the benefits of accountability, so I establish my expertise around accountability during the training.

If you aren't quite ready to present at events, or host your own, there are still many other ways you can position yourself as an expert. You can sponsor events, support events, or even just get your message and branding out there, during an event. You can write a book, or contribute to another's book. Participate in online forums; act as the expert. And, you must always blog. Blog, blog.

I sponsor events, either as a table sponsor where people can meet me in person and get to know what I offer, or I offer something to go into a give-away bag that each attendee will receive. I also offer laser-focused accountability coaching sessions to help people define the action steps they need to take to accomplish their goals.

One of the really successful things I've done is to contribute a chapter in a book related to my subject, like this chapter, where I can talk about how I position myself as an expert in Accountability – pretty cool! Of course, the next step is to write my own book and that is in the works.

I write blog posts offering tips on leveraging accountability and similar topics, and I ask and answer questions in forums where my target market hangs out. All of these things help me to be more visible and known as an expert in accountability.

Not everything works as expected

It's a bit hard to gain visibility as an expert in your chosen field when attending a local networking meeting or a big live event as a participant. You can only be in front of one or two people at a time. But, when you are a speaker or, even better, the host of an event, you are in front of everyone.

If you want people to see your articles, read your blog posts, and hear your podcasts, you have to market them; get them out in front of your potential clients. You need to know about keywords and SEO or you need to hire someone that does these things. Let them help you. Bottom line: no matter how much of an expert you are, you still need that visibility. Marketing is Key! Remember, you cannot be an expert if no one recognizes it but you.

Attending local networking events with other business owners in your community is a way to gain visibility and position yourself as an expert in your field, but you may not be in front of your ideal client or even your target market. It's better to attend an event, whether local or not, where the topic and focus of the event is something your target market is looking for and you know you can contribute. That way, you know whoever you meet at the event is potentially your ideal client or a possible Joint Venture partner (someone you may want to collaborate with on a project).

Always looking for new ideas

I've described what I have done and will continue to do to increase my expertise and position myself as an expert in accountability mentoring and coaching. Of course, everything tends to change over time so I am always on the lookout for new ideas that fit my background and, especially, my personality.

I explained previously that I have written chapters in two other books besides this one and now I am taking the next step to position myself as an expert by authoring my own book on the topic of accountability.

Summary

I hope you can see there are many, many ways to position yourself as an expert in your chosen field. I also hope you understand that one technique alone doesn't really work. It takes multiple approaches over time to boost your visibility and showcase your expertise.

I tried some methods that fell flat. So I dropped those and moved on to something new. I found what worked best for me and for my chosen topic and I continue to tweak that, while I try new ideas. You'll want to test all kinds of strategies for yourself and stick to what feels right for you and appeals to your audience. Your current and potential clients are the ones to listen to. They will let you know how they feel about what you are doing and saying. It was my clients, after all, that gave me the title "Queen of Accountability."

Known for her patient yet firm approach that holds your feet to the fire, Debbie's clients call her "The Queen of Accountability." As a former Project Manager, Debbie uses her planning and monitoring skills to teach you how to set Goals and Action Steps that stretch and keep you moving forward. In a loving and encouraging way, she mentors and guides you with practical insights and experienced suggestions to be productive, accomplish your goals, and build your own successful business.

Debbie conducts virtual Accountability and Coaching Programs for clients worldwide as she too travels the globe. Debbie also offers private 1-day intensive strategy sessions and group multi-day Glorious Global Gatherings in some of the world's most beautiful settings, like Ojochal in the southern Pacific region of Costa Rica. You can learn more about Debbie and her program offerings by visiting her site:

http://RevenueRecharge.com

What Does a Piano Have to Do With It?

By Eleanor Prior

Hi, my name Eleanor Prior and this is my story, Wife to McDreamy (12 years and he still has me whooped!) Crazy lady, as our five kids refer to me, AKA mom, in a blended family.

My background is in Social Media / Virtual Events and Affiliate Marketing. I'm a loyal die-hard WordPress.org fanatic and totally Geek on Internet Marketing!

Sometimes, I am delusional and pretend that I am the biological Kryptonian mother of Clark Kent; nothing is impossible for me to accomplish. I do have a kryptonite, make that multiple kryptonites: Wine and McDreamy.

Enough about me, let's get down to business. The business of "Positioning Yourself as an Expert".

"Never Forget That Even The Best Was Once A Beginner. Don't Be Afraid To Take That First Step To Greatness."

We are going to use the analogy of a pianist. No matter what age you start out at learning to play the piano, there are beginning steps you have to take. You first must learn your fingering, your fingers all have numbers: Your thumb is number #1, pointer is #2, tall man is #3, ring man is #4, and pinky is #5. The next thing you learn is the number of letters from the alphabet that are on the piano. There are 7: A, B, C, D, E, F, and G, along with the difference of the white and Black Keys (also known as twins and triplets). Then you learn how to locate the letters on the piano. For example D lives in the middle of a set of twins (two Black Keys).

From there you have your foundation built to become an expert. The same with becoming an expert online. You need to have your foundation built. So in order to position myself as an expert I took courses and built my foundation online which happens to live on WordPress, my personal website. This is my home online and where I want all my social media connections to eventually engage with me.

But it does not stop there, I can remember my piano teacher telling me "Practice Makes Perfect", "Use the right fingers", "Do that scale again", "Sit up straight", she was grooming me to become an expert so I could teach others.

My point is that no one is instantly an expert on anything. You have to study, learn and take action, aka practice what you have learned. One way would be by having content on your blog that is relevant to what you do online, and a glimpse of your personal life just to show you are human. Valuable content that is beneficial and teaches your audience to do something they might not know how to do.

I don't know anyone right off hand that started taking piano lessons and mastered the greats like Beethoven, Mozart, Chopin, Bach, Brahms, Debussy, Haydn, Rachmaninoff, Schumann, Strauss, Tchaikovsky, and many more. You won't be perfect but you will be mastering your craft. Adding content to your blog as mentioned above is only the beginning. So, no you won't be a Jason Fladlien, Wilson Mattos, Brian G. Johnson, Connie Ragen Green, Nicole Dean, Rachel Rofe, Dennis Becker, and many more overnight. But you will be you and people will seek you out for your expertise.

This has happened to me via my LinkedIn profile and I have enjoyed a couple of paid speaking gigs with the topic being social media.

Look, every piano student dreads their first recital unless they are a ham. But every student, after a successful performance, glows. You could say webinars, virtual events, Google hangouts, speaking engagements, can be likened to performing in recitals. These are some of the platforms I have used and use to position myself as an expert along with my website and social media profiles. Just like my first recital, I dreaded taking these steps, afraid of making mistakes publicly, but once my feet got wet I was hooked!

So if you were a pianist and wanted to position yourself as an expert, what would you be doing? You would be practicing your craft to perfect your skill. That is what I do on a daily basis. No, I don't practice my piano on a daily basis, although I should, this has been my former teacher's gripe along with my parents. But I do practice daily my skill sets as an online marketer.

I position myself as an expert by not being afraid to implement what I know and then share it with others. I find most people are very knowledgeable but allow FEAR to cripple them, myself included. So this is where you put your Big Girl / Big Boy Undies on and don't worry about failing. And say "take a hike False Evidence Appearing to be Real."

The more you fail the more you succeed, never be afraid to fail. My first webinar, I forgot to start it, so I was talking to myself. You will also find, while you think that you are failing, your tribe is growing and cheering you own.

Brace yourself, here comes another piano example. It would take me months to learn a Sonatina, to my teacher's dismay, but once I learned it, it was mine I owned it and it flowed perfectly. Let me tell you a secret that would frustrate my teacher to no end. I would have yearly exams to receive the next level certificates. She would fight with me to learn the songs and my theory for five months. Basically, I would wait to the last two weeks before my performance to practice and master my four pieces that would be performed for another teacher. I would pass with flying colors, but by the skin of my teeth. The other teacher who was evaluating me did not know that I had not been practicing for the five months.

My point, your audience will not know whether you have had this knowledge for years, months, or days.

Because it does not take years or months to learn a new skill online. If I don't have the skill, I am not afraid to part with some cash to learn the skill. Once I have mastered the skill I put it to use in my business.

To sum up what I have done and continue to do so I am positioning myself as an expert is learn, and then take action on what I have learned my implementing it in my business along with sharing my knowledge with others.

What am I doing to position myself as an expert in online marketing now?

I am continually learning and implementing new strategies. If I don't know how to do something I make it a goal to learn how to do it. I am not completely stubborn about this, however, if my time is best used elsewhere I will hire someone to complete one off tasks.

Also, if I find a service or a product I am offering no longer is in alignment with what I am doing, I kiss it goodbye and send it on its merry little way.

I love attending small live in person events. You will find that when meeting new people at these events you will have a lot to contribute to the conversation. This will establish you as an expert at the event. However, make sure you listen to others and enjoy their expertise. I learn so much from conversing with other attendees. Sometimes you might even be on the wrong path, or need constructive criticism.

Example: If you learn a song using the wrong fingering, you are always going to make a mistake. Mrs. Wasden would always lovingly chastise me. "Your fingering is incorrect, use the right finger!"

Maybe you are hitting the wrong note and don't know it, because you are so use to practicing it that way that is sounds correct to you. That wrong note you are hitting could cost you by taking away from your credibility.

If you are open for suggestions so you can improve you will grow and prosper. Just recently, one of my readers from my blog sent me a private note about the color of my text.

Hello:

I'd like to ask a favor: please use a higher-contrast text color so that people with vision problems can read your content easier. Currently, your style sheet indicates that you use #9da2a7 for your primary font and link color. For instance, It's almost impossible to see the email privacy link against the pink background of your contact submit button. Even a slight increase in the same blue-ish range would help greatly. May I suggest #898e92, or even better, #767a7e. Your audience is important. That light gray may seem ultra-cool, but it's also ultra-difficult for many viewers.

Thank you for taking a moment.

Now I could have been offended by this or ignored it. But I went to my site to view my light colored text. I was having a hard time myself with it. So I immediately copied and pasted the preferred text color he suggested.

This is the message I sent back to my reader:

Hello,

I like the suggestion and have made the change. I am even considering Black instead. Let me know what you think, if it is easier now. Thank you. I really appreciate the input I think the site looks better.

And to my delight this was the reader's response:

Golly, Eleanor....
Thanks for listening. I figured you'd take me for some kind of crank.
The change you made is great, so I wouldn't head for black text. It looks nice the way it is.
Hope you feel better soon.
cheers!

How did this help me position myself as an expert? It showed that I can be humble and welcome critics for improving. No one knows everything.

My social media profiles are another way I show my expertise, they are complete and I do my best to keep them up to date. Not to mention that I love to be everywhere and have multiples of most everything.

What Can I do in the future to further position myself as an expert?

Few things are as powerful or persuasive in business as becoming a recognized expert in your field. Let's go back to the pianist for a moment. One of my favorite things to play when I am being a brat with my husband, although I think it backfires on me and he enjoys it, is The Phantom of the Opera. Because at that moment I am passionately angry and I want to express it!

The duet between the Phantom and Christine is so powerful you can't help but feel the passion or be stirred from within. It changes your mood. I digress. What I am trying to say is that just as a song can be powerful, it can also be persuasive and so can we be when we are recognized experts in our field. Both You and I can be powerful, persuasive experts.

I mentioned at the outset that I am a diehard WordPress.org fanatic. Because of continually practicing my expertise this year, I was selected as a volunteer to run the social media for WordCamp Las Vegas 2014. This is just one example of a benefit you can enjoy when further positioning yourself as an expert.

So what can I do in the future to further position myself as an expert? Rinse and Repeat successful strategies. For example, I held a virtual event around Kindle in 2013. A benefit from this event was a brand new audience for me to engage with. This is something you can do yourself.

Continuing to learn, engage, implement and teach. "Practice Makes Perfect!" Just like a pianist, an expert is always practicing and performing.

On that note (catch my pun) I would like to end with this quote:

> *"...on the whole though I never arrived at the perfection I had been so ambitious of obtaining, but fell short of it, yet I was by the endeavor made a better and happier man than I otherwise should have been, if I had not attempted it."*
> *~ Benjamin Franklin (age 78)*

Benjamin Franklin positioned himself an expert with his accomplishments as a published author, inventor, musician, scientist, and more. Now ponder on this for a moment, he lived in a time period that did not have the advantages we have today, but he did not let that stop him.

I would like to invite you to my visit my foundation by visiting my WordPress site: http://eleanorprior.com
From there you can connect with me via my social media links. I will look forward to engaging with you.

Food For Thought

By Cheryl Major

My interest in all things health related probably began when my parents gave me a book when I was a toddler. The title was "Nurse Nancy", and although I don't remember the story, I do remember it came with Band-Aids, which I thought were very cool. As I recall, my mother had to replace the Band-Aids on a regular basis, and for a while my mom and dad suspected I might follow in my Aunt Frances' footsteps and become a nurse. That ended with high school science courses when I discovered I couldn't balance equations, and I managed to be out sick every time biology scheduled a dissection class.

Fast forward a couple of decades, and some health challenges led me down the path of researching better health through my food intake. The first book I read on this subject was "Sugar Blues" by William Dufty published back in 1975 which was a primer on the harmful effects of sugar on your body, appearance and general health. I had been diagnosed as severely hypoglycemic at the age of twenty-eight, and for a year I ate a very strict diet of three meals a day with three snacks in between. I counted and portioned what I ate, didn't eat sugar or white flour and didn't drink any caffeine or alcohol for over a year.

My efforts to position myself as an expert in the health field have been, until recently, accidental and have largely been forced upon me by necessity. As I have learned and discovered ways of eating that benefit me and improve my health, I have shared that information with those around me. In the mid 80s, my husband, whose family has a history of heart disease, discovered his cholesterol was high, so we went down the low fat diet path for quite a few years.

I am an animal lover, but I've never been a lover of eating meat, so when the healthy heart journey took meat off the menu, it was an easy one for me. In fact, except for poultry and fish, meat has not been on our plates for almost 30 years now.

The road to expert status in the realm of health and healthy eating has been a long one. Mostly trial and error, research and reading. The internet has given me a library at my fingertips, so there is always more information to assimilate, more food to try and incorporate into a healthy diet. In more recent times, in fact about a year and a half ago, my husband and I radically changed our eating regimen as a response to the side effects he was experiencing due to the mega doses of statins he had been on for seven years. Statins have only been prescribed for about the past 15 years, so the side effects are just coming to light now, and they are insidious! Neuropathy (which is extremely painful nerve damage), brain fog, weakness in the limbs, elevated sugar levels, cataracts, vivid nightmares, trouble sleeping and overall fatigue are just a few that are being reported. He decided to embark on a clean eating journey about a year and a half ago, and I signed on just to support him. Little did I know trying to help him would help me in ways that would change my life!

It is through this personal journey and experience that I have moved to position myself as an expert in the health and healthy eating field. I am not a doctor, so what I share with the people who come to me, and they do seek me out to ask me to share my experience, is just that...sharing my personal experience.

Together, my husband and I have succeeded, with the food we eat as our medicine, in normalizing his sugar levels. We each lost 20 pounds (without dieting), and I cured myself of decades of struggle with depression. I have more energy than ever before, and we love how we eat.

Most recently and going forward, I have decided to become certified in the health and fitness field. I am currently taking a course on nutrition to obtain my Nutrition & Wellness Consultant Certification (NWCC). This is not without its challenges. The books are huge, the print is small, and the amount of information to learn is massive! I feel as if I've taken on another college degree. The time commitment is also a challenge as I am a full time Residential Realtor and have been for over 25 years. I'm also committed to posting on my health blog on a regular basis and am writing a book about how I cured my depression using food as my medicine.

The decision to write the book was not an easy one as I am a very private person. To reveal my personal struggle and to let others take a look at the life I led for so many years as someone trying to hide the challenge of living with depression took some time to decide. The ultimate decision was based on my desire to help and was also based on my belief that modern medicine treats symptoms with prescription drugs rather than putting effort into prevention and solutions. My decision was also based on the realization, after much reading and research, that there is no percentage (read that as profit) in you and me being well or healing ourselves with food. Big pharma and modern medicine are in business to make money, not to help or heal with food. As callous and shocking as it sounds, cancer, diabetes and depression, just to name just a few, are big business.

Going forward, my efforts will include building a membership website where people can ask questions and share their challenges; where people can touch base if they want to eat clean, healthy food and see if it makes a difference in their lives. It's a tremendously simple and complex issue at the same time, and I find it endlessly fascinating!

I also will take my message to people through webinars and talks, which I enjoy giving. My hope is that when I have credentials in this field, my message will be taken more seriously.

Sometimes I worry that my intentions will be misconstrued as being biased toward thin people or biased against those who struggle with weight challenges. Neither could be further from the truth. I have only ever wanted to help people and to make a difference during my time here. For some strange reason, I was able to discover how to cure my debilitating depression with food. This has made such an amazing difference in my life that I want to share what has happened to me in the hope that it will help others lead healthier, happier lives.

I know there are forces in our world that are driven by money and by profit to the detriment of my fellow men, women, children, and also the animals around us...who matter to me greatly.

I intend to continue tilting at windmills for however long I am on this earth in the hope that I may make a difference in a life or two...maybe more. Maybe I can save someone from harm, improve the quality of a life, maybe give someone the ability to laugh and be happy because of how they have changed themselves by what they eat. This has happened to me, and I know I'm not the only one whose life can be recreated and uplifted by using food as medicine.

In my ongoing efforts to educate and share, I invite those reading this to follow my personal progress as I share an incredible, accidental journey that certainly changed my life, and may very well change yours!

http://ThinStrongHealthy.com is my website where I share as I learn. Join us there, take what you can use now, and come back often to grow with our community as we teach ourselves to eat well, love what we eat, and be happy! Live, love, laugh, and make Major improvements in your life!

The Innovation Expert

By Steve Sponseller

I am a husband, a dad, an animal lover, an outdoor enthusiast, and an innovation catalyst for many entrepreneurs and business leaders. I love spending time with my wife and twin daughters, as well as our dogs and cats. I enjoy being outside and surrounded by natural beauty, such as walking through a forest, hiking through the mountains, or sitting along the shore of a lake or ocean. A favorite place for our family vacations is the northern coast of California. The rugged coastline is beautiful and the energy of the ocean compliments the peaceful sounds of the waves, birds, and the breeze through the trees.

I am also an Electrical Engineer and an Intellectual Property attorney. I have enjoyed experimenting and learning how things work since I was a kid. One of my favorite activities in my childhood was taking things apart to see how they operated. As I got older, I learned to build things and design small projects with Lego and other materials. When the first personal computers were developed as I started high school, I fell in love with learning how to program them and discover how they operated. My early interest in discovering how things worked led me to study electrical engineering in college and, later, obtain a law degree.

During the past 20 years I have worked with over 1000 innovators and business leaders who have generated amazing ideas that are changing peoples' lives throughout the world. Those experiences have helped me position myself as an innovation expert. Although I did not intentionally set out to become an expert in innovation, my training and experiences naturally led me to obtain this status. I am now being more intentional about leveraging my expert status to continue building my own business and make a bigger impact.

I am grateful that today I continue my childhood joy of learning how things work and have the opportunity to interact with highly creative people every day. I enjoy the opportunity to see "what's next" – new products, new services, and new technologies that will improve the lives of many people. Few people get to see these coming attractions before they are released to the world because these new ideas are highly confidential during the development phase. Through my work as an Intellectual Property attorney, I have learned about business, problem solving, and innovative thinking. Most importantly, those experiences allow me to continue enjoying my childhood dreams of wanting to know how things work (and discover what's coming next).

I am now building my company, Innovation Strategies, Inc. to leverage my experience in working with so many innovative people. The company's mission is to teach business leaders how to discover and profit from the many innovative ideas hidden throughout their business. In my own business, I'm applying the same step-by-step innovation systems that I teach my clients. In essence, I am testing these innovation systems in my own business to help strengthen my status as an innovation expert. For example, my company leverages online automation tools that allow much of my business to operate on auto-pilot. I also follow the latest business trends and discover ways to leverage those trends to expand my own business.

The innovative design of my business allow me to manage all business activities from any location in the world. This gives me the flexibility to travel more frequently while still maintaining regular contact with my clients. I am not restricted to working in an office. Instead, I have the freedom to attend my kids' school activities and sporting events, participate in their hobbies, and be a positive influence in their lives. I also volunteer in my kids' classroom and help with field trips. The time flexibility offered by my business allows me to adjust my work schedule to accommodate the other activities in my life. I have also developed recorded programs that allow business leaders to learn about innovation at their own convenience by accessing the programs through the Internet.

I have positioned myself as an expert through a variety of activities. More than 20 years of work experience as an Electrical Engineer and an Intellectual Property attorney provides a strong platform for my expert status regarding innovation. My interaction with over 1000 innovators and business leaders at more than 100 different companies gives me a unique perspective. I have countless case studies detailing the innovation process and how businesses leverage innovative ideas to strengthen their company and distinguish themselves from their competition. By discovering trends and common systems among these case studies, I developed a step-by-step system that I teach my clients. I leverage these case studies regularly to teach "innovation lessons" that are applicable to many different industries.

Today I am strengthening my status as an innovation expert by continuing to work with innovators and creative thinkers every day. I am teaching clients how to identify innovation opportunities, develop innovative solutions, evaluate innovative ideas, and leverage the best ideas to grow their business. These clients are a wonderful source of referrals and testimonials that prove the value of my expertise.

I am continuing to learn new innovation techniques and study various trends that will impact a variety of businesses. For example, I attend seminars, subscribe to multiple trade journals, follow business blogs and podcasts, and receive daily alerts about innovation. After studying these new techniques and trends, I prepare my own articles, blog posts, and videos that discuss how businesses can take advantage of the techniques and trends. I also update my course materials to include these new techniques and trends so my clients always have access to the most up-to-date training.

Studying current trends and predicting how they will affect different industries is an important aspect of my innovation business. My clients rely on me to understand these trends and help guide them in analyzing how the trends will impact their own business both near-term and long-term.

I help them better understand the trends, then define brainstorming sessions and create "seed topics" to discuss during the brainstorming sessions. I may not be personally involved in all of the brainstorming sessions, but I help create the framework for successful sessions. These brainstorming sessions typically produce ideas for new products, enhanced product features, and other business innovations that distinguish the company from its competitors. This is an important part of the expertise I offer to clients – the ability to help clients discover various trends and then identify changes within their own business to take advantage of the trends.

To further strengthen my innovation expert status, I am a member of a mastermind group with several other business leaders and innovators. This group gives me the opportunity to help other business leaders leverage the latest innovation techniques to expand their own business and increase their competitive edge. These business leaders also provide valuable suggestions for my own business regarding how to position my expertise, how to attract new clients, and what types of training programs may benefit my clients. I have developed strong relationships with the members of the mastermind group, which validates my business ideas, provides valuable testimonials, and gives me a great sounding board for new ideas in my own business.

As I mentioned earlier, I prepare different types of information that I distribute publicly to increase my visibility to other business leaders. My blog posts and articles are focused on tips that teach people the basics of innovation. The questions and feedback I receive from these blog posts and articles keep me sharp, and enhances my learning. The feedback also gives me ideas for new course content and new training programs. I presume that if several people are asking similar questions about my articles or blog posts, there are likely hundreds or thousands of others with the same questions.

I schedule regular teleseminars to answer questions about innovation and provide an introduction to business innovation. These teleseminars allow people to interact with me directly and hear my voice. This is an important part of building a relationship with existing clients and prospective clients. And, the audio recording of the teleseminar allows individuals to listen to the recorded teleseminar at their convenience. In the future, I plan to create an innovation podcast that will allow people to subscribe to my teleseminar content and other audio information.

To continue building my expert status, I am working on articles related to business innovation that are being submitted to business publications and high-profile business blogs. I expect these articles to reach a large audience of business leaders who may not yet understand how their business can benefit from an innovation plan. For some of these publications, I hope to become a contributing author who writes a column or series of articles related to innovation.

Since I see great value in mastermind groups, I am going to create and lead a small innovation mastermind with 10-12 business leaders from different industry segments. Each member of the mastermind group will share their own innovation success stories and help other members of the group leverage innovation in their businesses. This will allow me to leverage my time, learn from others, and create a strong team of business leaders that supports one another. I will establish strong relationships with these business leaders that lets me better support their business growth and strengthens my position as an innovation expert in the business world.

I'm also excited to share my innovation knowledge with kids. I'm amazed at the creative ideas children develop in an almost effortless manner. Kids let their minds run freely without the limits and restrictions that hinder many adults. I am planning to develop programs to teach kids about innovation, how to focus their thoughts to produce valuable ideas, and further develop their ideas. Most importantly, I want to give kids a framework for solving problems and developing innovations that will continue to serve them in their adult life. Instead of having their creativity restricted as they get older, I am excited about the opportunity to have children enjoy a lifetime of creativity. I can't wait to see the innovations that today's children will develop to improve the lives of millions of people.

All of these activities and experiences position me as an innovation expert in the business community. I'm looking forward to strengthening my expert status so I can help more business leaders make a bigger impact in the world.

Steve Sponseller is an Innovation Strategist who teaches business leaders how to discover and profit from the gold mine of innovative ideas hidden throughout their business. You can contact Steve and learn about his step-by-step systems for identifying and developing innovations at:
http://www.InnovationExplained.com.

Things I Do Now To Position Myself as an Expert

By Adrienne Dupree

Current Tactics To Position Myself As An Expert

When I first thought about things I do to position myself as an expert, I drew a blank. I didn't really think of myself as an expert at least in the online marketing world. I am not a famous online marketer that everyone knows; however, I am doing things that are positioning myself as an expert. As I thought about it, I realized that I am doing a lot of things to position myself as an expert. The one thing you can do to position yourself as an expert is to seek visibility and deliver great content. There are many things that I am doing to position myself as an expert and so can you.

The first thing you can do is to blog on a consistent basis. If your blog contains great content, people will continue to come back to your blog and the search engines will start to rank your posts in the search engine rankings. Blog about things that are relevant to your niche. You can even ask your readers for topic suggestions. Be on the lookout for questions that they ask and others in your niche ask. These are great topics for blog posts.

You want a lot of content out on the Internet in a variety of formats. The best way to achieve this is to repurpose your content. Turn your blog posts into articles and post the articles on the article directories. You cannot just take a blog post and submit to the article directories. You need to completely rewrite it. Take several related blog posts and create a short report that you can give away. Encourage people to give it away so that it may become viral. Add links to affiliate products or your own products so you can monetize the report. Turn your blog posts into a PDF document and share it on the document sharing sites. Turn your blog posts into a PowerPoint presentation and share it on the file sharing sites. There are several document and file sharing sites that allow you to post your content for free. That same PowerPoint presentation can be turned into a video and shared on YouTube. You can then strip the audio and now you have another product. Audio can be shared on SoundCloud or turned into a Podcast that can be uploaded to iTunes.

You can also position yourself as an expert by participating in live events in your local area. One thing that you can do in your local area that is very easy is to start a

Meetup group that is related to your niche. I have done this for online marketing and we meet once a month at a local library. You can also hold a workshop in your area. I taught a ½ day Online Marketing workshop to insurance agents and network marketers. This could easily be turned into a ½ day workshop that is offered to the general public.

Don't just limit yourself to live events in your local area. Venture out and participate as a speaker in other live events that are out of town. You want to position yourself as an expert all over the country and the world. I have now participated in 2 events hosted by someone else on the other side of the country. I am exposing myself to different people and different events. Anytime you are speaking on a topic that you know something about, you are deemed as an expert in that particular subject.

Not only can you speak in person, but you can speak virtually. Teleseminars and webinars are two formats that you can use to position yourself as an expert virtually. I hold a teleseminar twice a month and I talk on different subjects that are related to my niche. I also provide a Study Guide that can be downloaded so the participants have something to follow. I leave the replay up until a few days before the next teleseminar to maximize the reach of the teleseminar. Webinars are also a great way to position yourself virtually. They should be used if you need to use slides for your presentation or if you need to actually demonstrate something. If you actually show your audience how to do something live then you are really positioning yourself as an expert.

It is one thing to promote other people's products, but you are seen completely differently when you have your own information products. You are then seen as a legitimate online marketer. In the beginning, create simple products. The products that I have created so far have been multi-media. They contain print, audio and video. I do this because some people are auditory learners and some are visual learners. I prefer to read and so do others. If you include all three, then you cover everyone.

Creating products with an online marketer that already has the traffic and visibility is a great way to get your name out there. I do not recommend that you just go around asking people if they would like to develop a product with you. Start to create genuine relationships with people and you will be surprised how many people will say yes.

If you really want to position yourself as an expert then become an author. When you say that you are an author you are seen in a different light. I suggest that you start with a Kindle book first. It is much easier to start with this format. If you are having difficulty coming up with enough material for the book yourself, then create a compilation book. Come up with a topic and then ask others to contribute a chapter to the book. My first Kindle book was created this way. At some point, you will want to publish a book where you provide all of the content. As I said, you should start with Kindle, but once you get your feet wet, you want to publish a physical book. A physical book is the ultimate business card. Instead of giving out a business card, you can give someone your book. How many business cards do you have that are stuffed somewhere in a drawer? If someone gave you a book, would you actually keep it and maybe even read it? Even if you don't read it, you would be impressed, wouldn't you?

The last thing I am currently doing to position myself as an expert is to submit press releases. You may not think you have anything newsworthy to report but you would be surprised. Every time I release a product I submit a press release. I was speaking at an event in Las Vegas and I submitted a press release. The local newspaper in my area picked the story up and wrote an article. Always have a "Google Alert" set up for your name so you don't miss when your name is mentioned.

Positioning Myself as an Expert in the Future

As you can see, I am well on my way to positioning myself as an expert, but there are many other things I can do. In some cases, there are things that I am not doing at all. Also, there are some things that I need to do more of and those are in my current plan.

It is easier to be a local celebrity or expert than a national one, but I am not currently doing the things I need to do to gain that notoriety. Sure, I am hosting a Meetup, but I need to do more. I could take that ½ day workshop that I did for the insurance agents and present it to other local small businesses. I could also take that workshop and turn it into a public workshop. I would need to find a venue, come up with a price, advertise and present my material. The slides are basically done so it would not take a lot to prepare. Once I feel comfortable with the workshops and I have a consistent following, I could then move to hosting my own events. I would start in my local area first because the logistics are easier. At some point, I could host events all over the United States.

I know that I need to create more content which includes short reports, articles, blog posts, webinars, teleseminars, YouTube videos and podcasts. I now have a plan for developing this content. I will create one short report a month, one article a week, one blog post a week, two YouTube videos a month, two teleseminars a month, two podcasts a month and two webinars a month. I believe that the webinars are something I really need to focus one because I have a lot of things that I can show my audience how to do.

Once you have at least 20 information products, then you are really seen as an expert. In order to achieve this, my plan is to create at least one information product a month. Once the product is completed, I need to actively market it and get affiliates to market it as well. If I can attract some big-time affiliates to promote my products, then that validates me as an expert.

Lastly, I really can't say enough about books. I am currently working on converting my Kindle book to a physical book and also working on my next physical book. I have so many ideas about book topics. My plan is to publish one physical book a quarter. I can't wait to go to my next live event with my books in hand. No more giving out business cards. Books will be my business cards for now on.

I believe if I stick to my plan and continue to do the things I am already doing to position myself as an expert and if I have the additional items from my plan, then I will be well on my way to being known as an online marketing expert.

Adrienne Dupree is currently a full-time Program Manager for a government contractor and a part-time online marketer. She has several information products and is also the author of "Leave The Corporate World Behind". She has a technical background with a B.S. in Mathematics, B.S. in Electrical Engineering and M.S. in Computer Science. The mission of her company, The Online Newbie, is to teach people in corporate America who want to get out the rat race how to stop trading time for dollars and be in control of their own destiny so that they can start an online marketing business. She is well equipped to help this audience because she is part of this community. She understands the pressures of having a demanding corporate full time job and how to balance it with a part-time online marketing business. To find out more about Adrienne Dupree and The Online Newbie and how you can leave the corporate world behind go to:
http://www.theonlinenewbie.com.

Becoming an Expert in My Niche: The Lost Item Identification and Recovery Service

By Boots Gibson

Becoming an "expert" in any niche is going to be different for each entrepreneur. In my case, it's taken several years and I'm still learning every day.

How Luggage Protection Tags Came About

Several years ago I saw a dateline TV segment about local burglars going to common carrier departure terminals (trains, buses, but mostly airlines) to get addresses off the luggage tags of people they knew were leaving town because they are in line in the departure terminals. Dateline called these people "Handle Surfers", using a play on a common term at the time, which was "shoulder surfers" - people looking over your shoulder to get your PIN code at ATMs.

The handle surfer would get in those long lines, the longer the better for their needs, act like a fellow traveler, and simply get those addresses as the lines would snake back and forth. They might possibly even learn how long the person would be gone by asking them as they chat in line—any "con person" can be quite charming as they chat with "fellow travelers".

Not long after seeing that show, I observed a fellow who seemed to be doing what they described in the Dateline program. He had a small carry-on bag which seemed to move very easily as if it had little or nothing in it. He was very friendly, chatting with most people as the line shifted back and forth for nearly an hour. He was in front of me in line at LAX (Los Angeles International Airport). When there was finally just a single person in front of him in the line, he asked me to hold his place so he could go to the bathroom. He then disappeared and never returned. I never saw him again. He was also on his cell phone often, typing something into the phone. Later I realized he could also have been photographing tags.

After this observation, I decided I needed to find a better way to ID my own luggage for future travel. While some travel gurus suggest using a home phone or cell phone number and/or an email on your luggage tags, my research led me to find out that home phones and even unlisted phone numbers can usually be Googled and the home address will quickly be found.

Then I started looking into lost and found ID service companies. I found several in the US, some in Australia, and others in Europe. They all seemed to have slightly different ways to approach the ID service and lost item recovery, but several had requirements I found quite distasteful to me. Thant's when I created a list of 8 points or "wants" in a service. This is that list:

1. If someone finds a lost item, I wanted them to be able to just pick up a phone and call me directly as if my own phone number was on that tag or label anytime 24/7. Even though smart phones seem to be everywhere these days, not everyone has easy access to a smart phone or to a computer for e-mailing, but most have access to a simple telephone and also know how to use it, especially if traveling in more remote areas.

2. I didn't want to have to wait while a Good Samaritan took the time to locate someone capable of using the internet and email to contact me. I didn't want to have to keep checking my computer for a notification to arrive. I didn't want to wait for a company to open their office and notify me during their limited office hours. I wanted a direct phone connection between me and the finder, and I wanted it in real time.

   Not a single company I could find offered the 24/7 direct phone connection.

3. Of course I wanted to know my contact information was protected from strangers at all times, even someone nice enough to try to return my lost item.

4. I wanted just a single ID number for everything IDed for the whole family, not individual numbers for each item, creating a nightmare of long ID numbers to keep track of.

5. I did NOT want to have to go onto a service's website and enter information about each and every item protect with an ID label or tag—that felt like an invasion of my privacy as well as a huge waste of time. Some were very detailed in the information they requested, like model number, purchase date and purchase price.

6. I wanted a single fixed cost to cover everything IDed. I didn't want to have to purchase huge numbers of small packets with just a few tags or labels in each packet to ID all the family's things.

7. I wanted to be able to make extra tags or labels in fun colors for kids or in different sizes than those offered, without being tied to a certain design and/or the expense of buying many extra packs of labels.

8. I wanted an easy way to remember the family's ID number and to have easy access to the company's contact information without having to carry a long list of ID numbers and contact info everywhere I went whether traveling to the local grocery store or across the country.

After looking at over 20 US based lost and found ID companies and finding none of them offered more than three of the items on my list, I decided others might be interested in the ID service I wanted as well, so I started Luggage Protection Tags, Inc. in early 2012. The following is the service that evolved from that list of "wants" for myself and my family:

- When someone finds a lost item bearing a Luggage Protection Tags label or key-tag, they call the 800 number enter your family's ID number when prompted to do so, and that call is connected directly and automatically to up to 4 of the member's own phones in real time.
- Each member's privacy is protected because even if the finder has caller ID, they see the company's phone number, never the member's number.
- Each membership kit includes 50 or 100 labels depending on membership level, but members are encouraged to make additional labels if they run out, if they want to save money, or they want their labels to have a different look, like special colors for their kids.
- Each membership includes either 1 or 2 ID numbers, depending on membership level. There is no long list of IDed items to keep track of.
- Each membership includes either 1 or 2 key-tags, which are important if you ever lose your keys, plus you always have the 800 number and your family's ID number right there in your hand if you ever have to contact us directly.
- There is never any need to go online and enter information on the items the member feels are important to protect—I think that's the member's business, not ours, so we don't have a database of your things.

When a member receives the call their lost item has been found, they can arrange to retrieve that item in a safe public place (like a police sub-station or in the main office at school for their kid's things) without giving the finder any personal info—you don't even have to give your real name if you don't want to.

If the recovered item needs to be shipped to you, have it shipped to a business address. Never give your home address. Even though the finder says they are in another area, they might be only a few miles from you and are trying to find you. You can have it shipped to trusted advisor with regular office hours for receipt of UPS or Fedex shipments. I have used my insurance man's office for such shipments for years.

The Business Evolved As I Learned More About My Niche

It became obvious, as my knowledge of our member's needs increased, that people deeded a way to protect everyday things other than just during travel times, especially kid's things. Protection Tags was another line that was added to the service. This really is the same service but was created for families with children that lost things in their day to day living. It's not just for those that are traveling long distances from home.

Child abduction protection specialists strongly advise against putting the child's name on things that can been seen easily by a stranger, like on their lunch boxes, backpacks, etc. Yet many schools require parents to ID their kid's things, especially for the younger kids in the early school years or nursery school.

Abductors can more easily make the child feel they are safe if the person uses their correct names. In addition, as we already learned, home phone numbers for ID are not safe because they can be traced to the home address. Protection Tags only have our 800 number, our website, and your family's ID number on them.

Protection Tags service gives a stranger easy access to call a parent if they find a lost item and want to return it, but they don't receive any info that can be used against any of your family members.

Neither parents nor kids have exclusivity in the ability to lose things; we all can easily drop something, or lay it down and walk of and leave an item behind and replacing them can be very expensive.

My Expertise is Still Growing

While I still feel I'm learning every day and finding new markets that need protection from unscrupulous people, I do feel I have reached a knowledge level that could be considered an "expert" in the lost and found ID and recovery world.

Boots Gibson has been a full time RVer for over 10 years and is all about travel as a lifestyle. She is a lifetime animal lover and animal advocate.

She worded in the medical field for 36 years as a respiratory therapist and later as a sleep tech for another 10 years. She has been online since the '80s when we had 5.25 inch floppy discs, internet access was fast at 1200 bod dial-up, because the real estate MLS service moved online. She has been out of real estate for many years.

Please visit at http://ProtectionTags.com or contact her on FaceBook, Linked-In, or Twitter.

How to Become an Authority Online

By Al Bargen

PHASE 1 - Gaining Expert Status in 'The Real World'

I timidly walked up the steps of the high school where I was about to attend my first martial arts class. It was hard to ignore the overwhelming feeling of butterflies in my stomach. I was only 11 years old then. I was instructed to quietly remove my shoes and put on my karate uniform. That first class was the pivotal moment in my life. Being there alongside other youths and adults, punching and kicking with the accompanying "Kiai!" hooked me. From that moment on, I knew I would always be involved in the martial arts.

Flash forward to over 10 years later. I was then an apprentice instructor of Jeet Kune Do or simply JKD. It was the natural next step in my martial art learning, but I was not yet fully aware that I was beginning to establish myself as an authority in my local community. I was in my early twenties and I shudder to think of myself as an expert at that time, although I had more experience and training that most others my age.

Previously, for almost four years, I trained with the brilliant martial artist Sensei Chris Taneda, a well-known karate expert in Canada. It was no accident that I had come under his tutelage. Seeing how the man deported himself and inspired his students fueled in me the desire to have the same kind of impact on my students. Looking back, I made the right move to seek instruction from the masters so that I may become an expert in the field of martial arts.

Training directly under the big names in the martial arts involved some travel. I remember feeling nervous when I, along with four other instructors, boarded a plane to Los Angeles. We had all paid big dollars for a full week of crazy training with Paul Vunak, one of the best JKD instructors in North America, and his right hand man, Tom Cruise. (No, not that one.) Over the next week, we were to undergo eight grueling hours per day of exhaustive martial arts training. I knew it was going to test us and stretch our capacities to the limit. Was this week in LA worth it? I'll never forget the last day. In pain and full of bruises but finally relaxing in a hot tub, my training partner Don and I were awarded our phase-one instructorship. It was the second rank in three levels of this "style of no style" martial arts.

Whatever it is you are pursuing, it can rarely be achieved sitting at home. You have to put yourself out there and suffer the bumps and bruises you will most certainly encounter along the way. Don't be afraid of them. It is these very bumps and bruises that make us strong. They create the dynamic of our individual being. Be adventurous. Be courageous. Facing your fear and acting in spite of it is how you gain knowledge and experience that will elevate you into expert status territory.

But in the realm of self-defense, what makes an expert?

This was the question I had for myself. I wasn't interested in competition or tournament fighting, the kind of fighting where no real contact is made. After some pondering, an answer came to me. An expert in self-defense is someone who has to defend himself in real life, against real attackers with no rules on a semi-regular basis. The easiest legal way to achieve this was for me to gain employment at a local bar as a bouncer. It lasted a year until I decided to branch out into more exciting security work.

I obtained a security license and went on to complete a series of bodyguard and semi-paramilitary trainings. After training with military trainers and other hard-core martial arts enthusiasts, I could perform just about any security task.

This was followed by many years of part-time event security peppered with some bodyguard and executive protection work. I worked for Bill Cosby, Cher, Elton John, Rod Stuart, Barenaked Ladies, Nickleback, and the list goes on. My role for these stars was not as a personal bodyguard. The goal was to work their events and eject the patrons who lost their privileges. I've been punched at, kicked at, grabbed from behind and attacked in different ways. At all times, I have defended against and dominated the attackers. I have never lost a physical altercation while performing my security duties. This I owe to having the single-minded approach to obtain the best training and experience to become a martial arts and self-defense authority.

I remember an incident during a high-energy 'The Offspring' concert. The youthful fans were screaming, moshing and drinking more than they were supposed to. There were many fights and more ejections. I was standing by the concession with two other security workers when, from out of nowhere, a large man sucker-punched my partner and was closing in on me. I thank God that I put in the work ahead of time. The crazed man who wanted to knock us all out was put to the ground hard and held for the authorities by myself. He was charged and convicted of assault.

With so many experiences like this, I knew I had achieved expert status in martial arts and self-defense. But there is a new challenge that exists – showing the world that I am who I say I am.

PHASE 2 - Gaining Expert Status Online - The Beginning

"Imagine earning all the money you ever thought possible – and all you had to do was create an info-product on your area of expertise and sell it online!"

Have you ever heard a pitch like this? I have and I swallowed it hook, line and sinker. Why couldn't it be possible? Many people were already doing it. Why couldn't I be one of them? I embraced the challenge, at least part of the time. For two and a half years, I played the online marketing game. What has been achieved? Well, it wasn't 60 days to 10k a month as the original product suggested, but I made some progress and continue to do so.

I have attained a great deal of expertise in the fitness and fat loss niches during the years training with mixed martial arts athletes and competitive fighters. Some of them were certified personal trainers and fitness experts. With the ideas I gained and exchanged with these experts, I was able to develop my own methods of maintaining six-pack abs and still be able to eat fat-laden food like cheeseburgers with relative frequency. I counselled others on my methods, which was the natural thing to do.

Below are just some of the things I have done in the grand effort to achieve expert status online.

I wrote a book.

Upon the advice of a branding expert and coach, I finally wrote and published *Cheeseburger Abs.* It felt amazing the day I held my first book in my hands and flipped through the pages. Writing a book alone has been one of the best action steps I have taken towards establishing authority status in the fat loss niche online.

I spoke on stage.

I received tremendously great feedback about my first time on stage that I forgot about how terrified I was to stand up there in the first place.

I received an award for my book.

Now, you may not recognize the award, but I stood on stage and proudly accepted it. This made me an "award-winning author," after all.

I received terrific endorsements.

I will never forget the evening in Toronto during a conference where I met Connie Green for the first time. I had the tremendous privilege to be sharing a glass of wine with New York Times bestselling sensation Dr. John Gray. I was asking him about the products he sold on his website and he asked to see my book. After a brief discussion, he grabbed it and signed an amazing endorsement in the inside cover. I couldn't believe my luck. I promise you one thing, you won't get that sort of 'luck' if you stay at home hiding behind your computer screen.

So why haven't I struck online gold yet?

Yes I did all those things, but I made mistakes along the way. I would get some great momentum, then stop the action. I would get a great endorsement like the Canadian Body For Life Transformation Champion sending me a video testimonial for the common sense approach and effective nature of my fat loss methods, and I sent no press release. Even the endorsement from Dr. John Gray received no press release or the special attention it deserved. Now the scope of this book is not so much about all the pitfalls, and mistakes we *can* make. It is how to gain expert status, so please learn from the above. When the iron is hot, strike!

PHASE 3 - Gaining Expert Status Online - The Future Strategy

Future's so bright, I need to wear shades.

Moving forward, I will be establishing my platform in both the fitness/fat loss niche and the martial arts niche. They are a natural fit. They complement each other. Learning from past mistakes and continually striving to better myself and my online marketing efforts, I am going to do a few things differently. I will examine the results of those changes, and course correct as needed. They are outlined below.

Here's the plan. Pay attention now, because this blueprint has been assembled with the help of some big names in the industry. Which parts can you adopt into your 'Authority Building Strategy?'

Write a book. (sound familiar?)

My second book on fat loss deals very specifically with the first 30 days of your commitment to change while you start out your fat loss journey. My first book covered many areas, and probably could have been a three part series. Learning from that, this next book will cover one topic... the first 30 days, and address it completely.

My first martial arts book on developing the mindset needed to face a potential violent encounter is in the proofing stage. I am very excited about "This Time It's For Real" and it's coming launch.

Conduct Interviews.

With one interview behind me, and 19 more to go, I have the frameworks for three more books pertaining to different aspects of self-defense and the martial arts. The questions I ask these martial arts masters are designed to round out these books. I will add my own thoughts, and experiences, and will also have my name, and picture up there, alongside these world renowned martial masters. How about that kind of association to build ones online authority?

Always have a coach.

I will always have coaches to guide me in my marketing efforts. The same is true in the martial world as well. I always strive to train with individuals that have more skill in at least one area. Don't stagnate. Continue to read and learn in your field. (Authority Building Hint)

Expand my Platform and reach with Social media.

This one has been a challenge, but I will put the pieces together this year. I will concentrate on the big five: Facebook, Twitter, Google +, YouTube and LinkedIn. Setting up profiles that look, and feel similar, then posting and engaging with people.

Be authentic in all I do online.

Maybe you felt that your writing online had to be perfect. Perhaps you felt as I did that your writing should leave everyone who reads it smiling, nodding their heads in agreement, and thinking you are simply wonderful. Come back to reality please. If Mother Theresa has haters, you will too. Imagine standing up and telling the world you can eat Cheeseburgers and look absolutely fabulous. I have had a few interesting comments. Ignore them, and don't even bother to engage the trolls online... those that just want to get a rise out of you. Do not engage the haters. (Sanity Saving Hint)

Continue to attend events.

Getting yourself out there is a crucial component in building authority status. Do it. You may even be fortunate enough to get invited to contribute to a future best-seller!

Maintain Relevant Memberships.

For me personally, memberships like WEBBS (World Elite Black Belt Society) are important. What memberships or associations would help you move upwards towards being an authority?

Continue to Post to blogs

Two times per week per blog (PLR re-writing is fine)

Continue to write articles for Ezinearticles.com

I am currently ranked 9 (thanks to Connie's advice) in the category of "martial arts" and will write, write and write some more until I am number one in the martial arts category.

Continue to post videos to YouTube

Simple short videos offering one complete thought are great. Don't over think it. I don't know how to edit, and it shows, but I am a regular guy out there not afraid to show that I don't have to know everything in order to succeed.

Start a Podcast

This scares me a little so I will start small. I am going to take the articles I have on Ezine and speak them. They won't be long, but they'll be a start.

Actually finish the sites I have online now.

You read that correct. I have a site for my fat loss book that doesn't even have all the bonuses I promised in the book uploaded to it yet. I have even sent the bonuses to a customer personally because of this unfinished site. The future holds complete sites.

Create some free reports out of some PLR or a few blog posts.

Do you have PLR in a folder somewhere collecting "e-dust?" Me too. I am planning to challenge myself to take the time required and create some engaging free reports.

Finally edit the workout footage I have to market fitness videos of my own.

This is self-explanatory.

Create many e-books on self-defense topics like travel safety tips, securing your home. Did I mention I took a locksmith course with this book in mind just to establish authority?

Connect with like-minded individuals and potential JV partners.

All the things I plan to do online have an affiliate marketing component to them. Establishing these relationships early, and in person is the best way to secure this intention.

Rome wasn't built in a day. One foot in front of the other. A journey of a thousand miles...

Authority status, or transforming into an expert online does not happen overnight. Grab your favorite cliché above and embrace it. The main things to remember are that you can't fail if you don't give up. And that you will achieve your online goals if you simply persist.

> *"Never consider the possibility of failure;*
> *as long as you persist, you will be successful."*
> *~Brian Tracy*

Al Bargen is a fitness and fat loss expert, consumer advocate, accomplished martial artist, and insatiable adventurer.

Some of his achievements are...

... writing Cheeseburger ABS: Eat What You Want and Look Absolutely Fabulous, your ultimate guide to eating what you want and getting the results you deserve.

... attaining black belts in three different styles of martial arts, including a second degree black belt in Jishin-Ryu Jiu-jisu, and Phase one instructor status in Bruce Lee's Jeet Kune Do

... exploring the rugged wilderness of his native Canada every year, by hiking and sightseeing

... teaching his clients to be the best they can be by sharing knowledge of personal fitness that has been gained over a lifetime.

... overcoming difficult experiences, like abdominal surgery, and training back to peak fitness

... establishing the website ModernSamuraiSociety.com

Growing and Positioning Yourself as an Expert

By Leslie Ann Cardinal

When you think about "positioning yourself as an expert" do you sometimes feel a bit uncomfortable to proclaim yourself to be an expert? Are you concerned that it might be too much like bragging? I'm Leslie Ann Cardinal and I have to admit that I had some of these thoughts when I first encountered the idea of positioning myself as an expert. So I would like to share some ideas and thoughts with you from my experience, that I hope with help you as you begin to position yourself as an expert. I'd like to put your mind at ease about this in the same way that I did for myself, by shifting your thoughts about it slightly. And I want to help you do this in a way that I believe will serve you well, that will serve other people well, and that will help you to grow your business, too.

There are three main topics I'll cover in this chapter. The first is about getting comfortable seeing yourself as an expert. The second is about growing yourself as an expert. And the third is about positioning yourself as an expert in the larger world.

Let's start with the first one, getting comfortable with seeing yourself as an expert. Here is what I have learned: when you use the word "expert," it just means that you are a person who has knowledge and experience that can be helpful to other people. You may not be the most advanced expert. In fact, there will almost always be people who know more than you do, or who have more experience than you do. But you DO have knowledge and experience, and if you are willing to share it in a way that helps others, that it what really matters.

In fact, it can be better not to be too far ahead of the people you will be leading or assisting. You can more readily remember what it is like to be where they are in the development process. You can remember the difficulties and the challenges you encountered. You can remember how good it feels to make progress and to learn each step. You can remember the courage and energy it takes to move forward too, and you can help people with this knowledge. The methods you used to learn and to grow may still be very relevant to someone else who is learning, compared to an expert who mastered the skill many years or even decades before.

So, to begin the process of positioning yourself to be known and perceived as an expert, start with your own inner work about being an expert. This means building your confidence that you do, in fact, have knowledge and experience that can be helpful to other people. I will share with you some of the methods I have used to build my inner confidence, so that you can use these methods yourself.

Make a list of the topics that you have some knowledge about. It will likely be a long list. Make another list of the experiences you have had using and applying your knowledge. These lists can include things from your work experiences as well as from your personal life experiences. I recommend that you write these lists in a notebook or start a computer file, so you can go back and add to the lists and use the information later to give you examples to draw upon.

Now ask yourself if you would be willing to share some of your knowledge and experience if it could help someone else. I have found that the more I am willing to share my knowledge and experience to help other people, the more joy and confidence I have in my own expertise. Your willingness to share your experience and knowledge to help others and the feedback you receive can help to build your confidence too.

You can also approach this process from the other side: What have you enjoyed helping people with in the past? When have you given directions or answered questions or shown someone how to do something? What topics would you enjoy helping other people with in the future? Your answers to these questions will give you a good start in identifying one or two best areas where you can begin to position yourself to be known as an expert now.

The second important characteristic of an expert is that they continue to learn and grow. This is so important, because of the ongoing changes and updates in all fields. Part of being an expert is actively taking steps to keep learning more about your area of expertise, and to keep expanding your depth and variety of experience. The extra benefit of doing this is that the more you learn and grow your expertise, the more your confidence as an expert will to grow too.

Make a commitment to keep growing and learning. One of the ways I do this is to always be working with a good coach or a mentor. I recommend that you do this too. When you look for a good mentor or coach, look for someone who can guide your ongoing growth, and who can even accelerate your development. A coach can help you stay on track and focused. They can often introduce you to their network of resources and contacts which can be very helpful to you in building your expert status.

In addition to working with a coach or mentor, some of my other favorite ways to keep growing my expertise include classes, reading, listening to audiobooks and podcasts of interviews with other experts, and going to conferences and live events. My goals is to always have at least one or two of these things that I am doing to learn and grow my expertise. I encourage you to adopt this practice too.

The third key aspect of being an expert is to begin to actively convey yourself as an expert. This doesn't mean being aggressive or pushy. It just means allowing others to know that you have knowledge and experience. Meetings and workshops and live events are great places for this to start to happen.

I have found live events to be so valuable for positioning myself as an expert that I want to go into more detail about them and how you can benefit from them too. There are three main types of events that will be useful to you when you are building your expertise and later as you are positioning yourself as an expert. First, look for meetings and events in your own professional field. Second, look for meetings and events focused on business skills and business development. And, third, look for events in the fields of your favorite types of clients.

For example, I work with successful women in their 50s and 60s to help them continue to achieve new levels of business and professional success. My special fields of knowledge and expertise include coaching and training people about business and career success. So, I go to events for coaches and for training and development professionals. I also go to business growth and development events sponsored by groups such as Chambers of Commerce, women's business groups, and events about online business development. In addition, I look for opportunities to speak at meetings where my ideal clients often go, such as meetings for professional women in fields like nutrition, real estate, insurance, health care and holistic health, accounting, and technology.

To find events and groups in your area, you can use Google to start your search. Look for local business associations and Chambers of Commerce. These types of groups will have events every month that you can attend as a visitor. You can also look for local Meetup groups that focus on business and on your special areas of expertise. Look for business networking groups such as BNI, Goldstar, and LeTips groups, too. You can go as a visitor to most groups and meet a variety of people.

I have found that one of the secrets of success with this is to be steady in attending events and groups over time.

Allocate time and money for attending events and attend as many as one or two local meetings each week. You don't have to attend a group's meetings every time, but don't just go one time and expect to come away with instant clients and recognition. It takes time for people to get to know you and to see that you are someone who regularly participates in events and meetings.

Visit a wide variety of groups to see what is available in your area. Also, look for live events that may be further away, but which will draw a larger group or that will provide more in depth training. These can include conferences and workshops led by other experts in your field. Look for groups that have useful educational programs and that attract the types of people who could potentially be good clients for you or who could possibly refer good clients to you. Over time, you may be able to become one of the speakers or presenters at these groups, further positioning yourself as an expert.

Eventually, you may want to actually become a member of one or two business or professional groups and to get involved on a deeper level. Volunteer to help with a committee or to assist one of the leaders with some of the tasks of running the group. This is always appreciated in any organization. It will help you to build stronger and deeper relationships with other members of the group. It will also help others to begin to know you, to like you, and to trust you. This can lay the foundation for future referrals, for joint ventures, and for other opportunities for you.

Be open to being a mentor in your field as you grow in your experience and knowledge. I have found this to be very rewarding and I hope you will find it to be valuable too. Be willing to talk with others who may be interested in joining your field, and to people who are new to your profession. Be willing to answer questions and to connect people to helpful resources. When you meet people, ask if there is anything that would help them that you might be able to connect them with, such as resources, ideas, solutions, or other people. Exchange business cards or contact information and suggest staying in touch with them.

If you are in any type of service business such as coaching or training or consulting, it is especially beneficial for people to meet you in person, to hear you, to shake your hand, and to hear your ideas. This enables them to get to know you more directly and to sense if they like you and feel a potential connection with you. I have found that this can lead to doing business together, or to referrals, over time. Whether you are mixing and mingling at a networking event, or speaking to a group, or participating in a workshop or event, the opportunity to meet in person can be very powerful for positioning yourself as an expert.

Another great way to position yourself as an expert is to do some type of public speaking for groups, preferably about your topic of expertise. This could include speaking to professional associations, Chamber of Commerce groups, and Meetup groups. Speaking is one of the fastest ways for people to get a sense of your style and knowledge and expertise.

If you have not done a lot of public speaking, it is worth the effort to learn this skill. You can learn to speak capably in public by attending Toastmasters meetings, taking classes, and by practicing and getting feedback. At Toastmasters you will receive great training and friendly encouragement and support whether you are a novice speaker or have a lot of experience.

There are many groups that need a speaker for every meeting. They are always looking for speakers and you can help them out by contacting them and offering to speak. Ask about the types of topics their members enjoy and look for ways to connect these ideas to your area of expertise. Be ready to suggest a topic or two that you could speak about, if necessary.

When you speak for a group, write a short introduction so that the person who will introduce you can use it rather than trying to come up with something on their own. Include information about your expertise. It is very easy and natural for them to give you a very nice introduction that highlights your expertise because they will be the one saying it and not you.

Every time you speak, ask the organizers of the meeting if they know of other groups that could use a speaker too. You can often get referrals to one or two additional places to speak every time you give a talk. And being able to say that someone suggested that you contact them about the possibility of speaking is another great way to position yourself as an expert.

There are many additional related ways to be visible and to position yourself as an expert. You can be listed in directories of groups you belong to, you can participate in community and charitable events, and you can list yourself with referral services.

So, in summary, you really do have knowledge and experience that can help people. You can continue to grow your knowledge and expertise which will grow your confidence as an expert too. And you can take specific steps to actively position yourself as an expert. I hope that you will do this because there are people just waiting to learn from you and to benefit from your services. When you take the leap to see yourself as an expert and to position yourself as an expert, you can truly make a difference in the world.

Leslie Ann Cardinal coaches and teaches women professionals who are "50 and better," helping them to reach new levels of business and personal success. She has been coaching and teaching success principles for more than 25 years. You can learn more about her at:
www.GrowYourBusinessNow.com.

Jack Of All Trades, Master Of... One?

By Geoff Hoff

I know a little bit about a lot of stuff. For those subjects, I am a dilettante. Webster's Dictionary defines dilettante as a person whose interest in an area of knowledge is not very deep or serious. There are a few things that I know a lot about. For most of them, I don't think I'd call myself an expert, although Webster's defines that as a person who has special skill or knowledge relating to a particular subject, which, I imagine, qualifies me to use the word.

I see a lot of dilettantes passing themselves off as experts. I have been guilty of it myself, I'm afraid.

When I was growing up in the small, northern New Jersey town of Flatbrookville, there was a local fellow who did odd jobs. He was what we would now call a handy man. I would often see him puttering around my grandparents' inn, fixing broken windows, painting the rest room floors, installing Grandma's flower boxes, etc. I heard my grandfather refer to him as a "jack of all trades, master of none."

Grandpa was implying that he wasn't an expert painter or glazier (someone who installs glass windows) or carpenter. He was good at those things, but not really an expert. This man seemed to me, though, a kind of miracle man, someone who could do anything, and do it well. In a small town like Flatbrookville, you didn't necessarily have enough work for a full-time, expert electrician or glazier or carpenter, so this fellow was who people would call. He obviously enjoyed his work and did it well enough.

I grew up being interested in many, many things. I loved reading, movies, drawing and painting. I also loved nature, science, gardening. In high school, I discovered organic chemistry and was enthralled. In college, it was imaginary numbers. I was fascinated by mechanical things, by electronic things. I loved language and languages. I was moved by people who did things that seemed to shape and change the world around them. It didn't matter if it was in a local, national or global way. I loved animals. I loved magic; the kind involving black hats, scarves and lovely assistants, the kind you read about in books with dragons and wizards in them and the "every day" magic of a profound connection with someone or an ephemeral and imperfect glimpse into the near future. I loved the magic that science gives us. Things like imaginary numbers and string theory and broadcast television and computers.

I investigated all of these things, one way or another, but, from a very early age, I told stories. I wrote my first short story when I was nine. A year or so later, I wrote a script for the original Star Trek TV show. It wasn't very good, but my mother typed it out for me and kept it in the front of her huge dictionary until the day she died. All the other things I was fascinated with became secondary to writing, and fed the writing.

As I entered the workforce in earnest, I took what work I could find. I mowed lawns and slung pizzas. I served soda and wine coolers. I spent time as a picture framer, then moved to answering phones, then to a mail room, to a file room and back to another mail room. I was asked to step in temporarily when the computer guy at a law firm I worked for had to leave and they didn't have anyone to replace him, so I became a tech guy. I learned each job and did each one well. (Except, maybe, that short stint as a phone salesman. I sucked at that.)

The whole time, though, on my own, I wrote. I wrote in the evenings and on weekends. I wrote at lunch and, when the job had them, during down times. I wrote stories and poems and novels. I wrote articles and essays, opinion pieces and humor pieces. I studied writing, and, more deeply than that, the process of creativity itself. I studied it not like a college student would, but as a life's work. I observed and compared and asked questions and read and experimented.

This study was so much a part of me that I didn't even realize it was study. I didn't even realize that most people didn't spend their time contemplating these things.

I wrote a book about writing, using short stories as the form, and sold it online as an eBook. The first course I ever taught online was a short story writing course based on that book. Most of the participants in that course wrote short stories during it. For many of them, it was their first. And for many of them, they continued on to write more. One actually sold the story she'd written in the class. She sold it to a literary magazine, and wrote to tell me so in an email that was infused with glee.

I took what I'd discovered teaching that class, added it to the original book and published it on Kindle.

And, yet, I hesitated to call myself a writing expert. I felt like that handy man back in Flatbrookville. Good at a lot, great at nothing. I could hear my grandfather say, "jack of all trades... " and it stopped me short. But I began to know that I actually did have some expertise. When I was discussing creativity or writing, I did know what I was talking about. My students were actually able to use what I taught them and use it, sometimes, quite powerfully. They were able to make it their own, which, as far as I'm concerned, is the best and most profound compliment.

It was a huge leap of faith and courage when I was finally willing to use that word in regard to myself about anything I'd ever done: expert. It was kind of a surprise when I discovered there were people who already thought of me that way, as a writing expert. When people think of you as the one who knows about a subject, you are already an expert, whether you think so or not.

When you begin to realize you do have the knowledge and experience, that your knowledge and experience can actually benefit others, actually calling yourself an expert can make a big difference. And then getting your knowledge out into the world so more and more people will see you are the expert will help more and more people. There are many ways to do this. You'll probably read about some of them in this book. I imagine writing blog posts, articles and press releases will be among the ways mentioned. Making videos and publishing books, networking among your fellow experts and among the people who want what you have to offer will probably have been examined. Some of these I do, some, not as much as I should, some I don't. A few will be right for you, some, maybe not. That's not important, ultimately.

What is important is seeing that you do, indeed, fit the definition of expert; a person who has special skill or knowledge relating to a particular subject. Then, once you see that, start to think of yourself that way, than let others in on the secret however you can. People want to do business with those they see as having special knowledge. They want to learn from people who have made a deep study and practice of the subject. When you are that person, and you let people know that, they will want to do business with and study with you.

And that handy man? He was, actually, a master. He was an expert handy man. He was the one man, in the whole valley and surrounding area, that people contacted when they needed stuff done around their houses and farms. The whole "master of none" was his expertise. He could do whatever you needed done, and he could do it well.

Geoff Hoff is President and COO of Hunter's Moon Publishing, a company he created with Connie Ragen Green to help entrepreneurs write and publish books in order to enhance their credibility, grow their audience and be recognized as authorities in their field. He is a best-selling author and has been an actor, acting teacher, standup comic and popular blogger and teaches courses in both creativity and in tech on the Internet.

You can find him at http://GeoffHoff.com When you visit his site, be sure to pick up his free report on what inspiration really is and how you can harness it for yourself and your business.

Positioning Yourself as an Expert

By Connie Ragen Green

In 2005 I came to the conclusion that I was not living the life God had intended for me. This stark realization manifested itself in my desperately wanting to leave my current life behind and start anew. It wasn't that I was unhappy; it was more of a feeling that I could do so much more if only I had the time and money to do so. Also, I dreamed of being able to volunteer my time in my community and to help raise money for charitable organizations.

I began to search for something I could do from home to replace my income as a classroom teacher and real estate broker/appraiser and soon found that people just like me were running successful businesses from their home computers. I was aware that large corporations such as J.C.

Penney and Sears were selling and doing business online, but finding out that individuals were doing this on a much smaller basis was a concept I had not yet heard about.

You know that feeling of excitement you get when you come upon something that resonates with you in a huge way? That's exactly how I felt when I heard about online entrepreneurship. Once this idea came into my realm of consciousness I knew that I'd be willing to do whatever it would take to get my own business up and running successfully.

Over the next year I learned as much as I could and took immediate action on everything that was recommended to me. In the process I connected with people from all over the world who were also doing this, and that's when my self-doubt began to come on strong. Even though I believed I could do this and be successful, each day I felt more and more like a fraud. It seemed that everyone else was smarter, more experienced, and already known in their niche and that I was never going to be an expert in anything having to do with business.

At the end of 2006 I had to make a choice; was I going to give up on my dream because I felt like I had nothing to offer, or simply move forward and position myself as an expert? I chose the latter and made sure I did at least one thing every single day to get my name out to the world. I was willing to do whatever it would take to change my life and become a successful entrepreneur. I didn't expect this to be an easy undertaking, but little did I know it would be work I would love so much.

Here are the steps I took over the next couple of years that helped me to stand out in my field with a unique voice:

- Chose the niche of eBook writing and marketing because of my previous experiences in helping students to write in the classroom. It was my belief that this was a way I could serve others in a meaningful way while I was learning exactly what to do in my new online business.
- Wrote my own eBook on real estate marketing on the Internet, a topic I was learning about as a new online entrepreneur. This helped me to leverage knowledge I already had with new strategies I was learning.
- Started blogging regularly about my areas of knowledge and expertise, including eBooks, residential real estate, small dogs, and becoming a new online entrepreneur.
- Wrote an article every day on one of these topics and submitted it to the free article directories. The blogging and article writing turned me into a writer and got me into the habit of writing every day.
- Started recommending the products and courses that were helping me to find others who wanted to get started, using my affiliate link. This put me on the path to 'earning while I learned'.
- Created several of my own information products, based on what was working for me. These included trainings on blogging, article marketing, and using technology in your business. I've always believed that if you are able to teach someone else what you know, that means you know it thoroughly, inside and out.
- Attended as many teleseminars as I could, making sure to arrive early so I could introduce myself and

give my website url. As long as I was learning from other online entrepreneurs, I figured I might as well connect with the other attendees. This was before social media, so this was especially helpful with meeting other like-minded individuals.

- Began going to local events in my community (Rotary, Chamber of Commerce, library meetings, community events, other charities) and telling anyone who would listen who I was and what I did to serve others in my new online business.

These eight steps gave me great traction, online and offline, and also helped build my confidence that what I was doing was meaningful to others and something they would be willing to pay for so they could achieve similar results. You may have noticed a theme to these steps; they each involve 'learning' or 'teaching'.

By 2009 my business had grown more than I ever had imagined it could. It was then that I made the conscious decision to take it to the next level. I wrote out a plan of which activities I would engage in actions I would take to ensure that I would be positioning myself as an expert in my field and increasing both my credibility and my visibility in the process.

These activities included:

- Attending as many marketing and business events as possible, even if they were in other countries. At first I was an attendee, but was soon invited to speak and present on my topics. This led to my being invited to speak in Canada, the United Kingdom, and even in Thailand.

- Hosting my own live events. I first did this with a partner, Dr. Jeanette Cates, and later on my own with my Weekend Marketer Live workshops, which I continue to host twice a year.

- Reading as many books as possible on the topics of business, marketing, leadership, and entrepreneurship to give myself the business education I was lacking in my life experience and formal education.

- Writing and publishing books on my topic, and making sure to publish one new book each calendar year. I am currently working on my tenth book, *The Transformational Entrepreneur*.

- Starting my own publishing company, Hunter's Moon Publishing to have more control over my writing.

- Going out of my way to connect with thought leaders in the online marketing space to learn from them and to share my own thoughts and ideas with them.

- Taking action with something every single day, three hundred sixty-five days a year, to further my business. Some of this can be delegated and other tasks can be automated, but having a hands-on approach to your business and thinking about it each day will make a huge difference in your overall results.

These seven activities have helped me to grow my business even further over the past several years and have taught me so much that I would have otherwise missed while I was busy with the day to day activities of running a business.

So, what does the future hold for me as I continue my quest to better position myself as an expert and an authority in my field? Hindsight is always twenty-twenty, so knowing which direction to take at your present point in time is always the big question.

I believe that the competition among those doing business on the Internet will continue to increase, and that we must all put our best foot forward in order to enjoy the credibility that brings new prospects and clients. These are the steps I have started taking to ensure that my expert status continues to grow over the next few years.

- I'll make sure that all of my websites look and feel professional. The days of 'homemade' sites put together using a program such as FrontPage are long gone, so insist that the tech person helping you knows how to create sites that represent you as a knowledgeable expert and authority in your field.

- Channels will set you apart from others in your niche, and these include YouTube, iTunes, Amazon, and social media. I'll continue to add new videos, podcasts, books, and relevant posts so that visitors to my channels will know who I am and what I have to offer them that will help them to achieve their own goals.

- There is no real substitute for connecting with people in person, so I will continue to attend, speak at, and host live events in a variety of locations all over the world. This will enable me to meet more people face to face who are on a similar path as myself, and to invite them into my inner circle of friends, colleagues, and associates. I have found that nothing dampens your spirits and causes you to have self-doubt more than spending time with people who do not understand and live the path to success. Surround yourself with do-ers and action takers who understand how to leverage the power of the Internet to increase your bottom line exponentially.

Take a closer look at where you are right at this moment, both personally and professionally to see which steps make sense for you to engage in. If you do not have the time and financial resources you desire as an entrepreneur, it is definitely worth your while to make the effort to position yourself as an expert now.

Connie Ragen Green is an online marketing strategist, multiple bestselling author, and international speaker living in southern California. Find out more on how she can help you move forward by visiting http://ConnieRagenGreen.com.